Age, race and ethnicity

RETHINKING AGEING SERIES

Series editor: Brian Gearing
Department of Health and Social Welfare
The Open University

The rapid growth in ageing populations in Britain and other countries has led to a dramatic increase in academic and professional interest in the subject. Over the past decade this has led to the publication of many research studies which have stimulated new ideas and fresh approaches to understanding old age. At the same time, there has been concern about continued neglect of ageing and old age in the education and professional training of most workers in health and social services, and about inadequate dissemination of the new information and ideas about ageing to a wider public.

This series aims to fill a gap in the market for accessible, up-to-date studies of important issues in ageing. Each book will focus on a topic of current concern addressing two fundamental questions: what is known about this topic? And what are the policy, service and practice implications of our knowledge? Authors will be encouraged to develop their own ideas, drawing on case material, and their own research, professional or personal experience. The books will be interdisciplinary, and written in clear, non-technical language which will appeal to a broad range of students, academics and professionals with a common interest in ageing and age care.

Current and forthcoming titles:
Simon Biggs and Chris Phillipson: **Elder abuse in perspective**
Ken Blakemore and Margaret Boneham: **Age, race and ethnicity:**
   A comparative approach
Joanna Bornat (ed.): **Reminiscence reviewed: Evaluations,**
   achievements, perspectives
Bill Bytheway: **Ageism**
Julia Johnson: **Structured dependency and older people**
Moira Sidell: **Health in later life: Unravelling the mystery**
Christina Victor: **Rethinking community care for older people**

Age, race and ethnicity
A comparative approach

KEN BLAKEMORE
and
MARGARET BONEHAM

OPEN UNIVERSITY PRESS
Buckingham · Philadelphia

Open University Press
Celtic Court
22 Ballmoor
Buckingham
MK18 1XW

and
1900 Frost Road, Suite 101
Bristol, PA 19007, USA

First Published 1994

A catalogue record of this book is available from the British Library

ISBN 0 335 19086 3 (pb) 0 335 19234 3 (hb)

Library of Congress Catalog number is available

Typeset by Type Study, Scarborough
Printed in Great Britain by Biddles Limited, Guildford and Kings Lynn

Hold! Stop your sympathy!
Understanding if you got it,
Otherwise I'll do without!

From 'On Aging', by
Maya Angelou (1986)

Contents

Series editor's preface

The rapid growth in ageing populations in Britain and other countries has led to a dramatic increase in academic and professional interest in gerontology. Since the mid-1970s we have seen a steady increase in the publication of British research studies which have attempted to define and describe the characteristics and needs of older people. Equally significant have been the very few theoretical attempts to re-conceptualize what old age means and to explore new ways in which we think about older people (e.g. Johnson 1976; Townsend 1981; Walker 1981). These two broad approaches which can be found in the literature on ageing – the descriptive (what do we now know about older people?) and the theoretical (what do we understand about older people? And what does old age mean to *them*?) – can also be found in the small number of post-graduate and professional training courses in gerontology which are principally intended for those who work with older people in the health and social services.

Concurrent with this growth in research and knowledge, however, has been a growing concern about the neglect of ageing and old age in the education and basic training of most workers in the health and social services, and about inadequate dissemination of the new information and ideas about ageing to lay carers and a wider public.

There is, therefore, a widening gap between what we now know and understand about ageing and ageing populations and the limited amount of knowledge and information which is readily available and accessible to the growing number of professional and voluntary workers and others who are involved in the care of older people.

The main aim of the *Rethinking Ageing* series is to fill this gap with books which will focus on a topic of current concern or interest in ageing. These will include: elder abuse; health and illness in later life; community care; and working with older people. Each book will address two fundamental questions: what is known about this topic? And what are the policy and practice implications of this knowledge?

It is timely and significant that the first title in a series on rethinking ageing should be *Age, Race and Ethnicity*. The importance of this topic has not been adequately reflected in the gerontological literature and, as Ken Blakemore and Margaret Boneham observe in their Introduction, the ageing of Britain's black and Asian older people has not been high on the agenda for either social research or for consideration by policy-makers in the health and social services. In marked contrast to the extensive social policy literature which deals with issues of racial discrimination, crime and black–white relations, there have been only a very few studies of *older* Afro-Caribbeans and Asians in Britain. As the authors point out in Chapter 2, if we are interested in a national picture of how older Asians, Afro-Caribbeans or other minority elders are faring, research has hardly begun and a similar ignorance pervades our view of relations between older members of minorities and health and social service providers.

The significance of this book on race and old age in Britain therefore lies in the way it brings together in one volume all the major research studies and literature on older Asian and Afro-Caribbean people, along with some theoretical material of the authors which will be of interest to those working with older people in the health, social work, education and race relations fields. This book also represents an important first attempt to relate the literature on race and ethnicity, including the authors' own research, to theory and practice in gerontology, which for too long has been largely ethnocentric, if not colour blind.

A particular strength of the book is the emphasis placed by Blakemore and Boneham on the diversity to be found among Asian and Afro-Caribbean people. This diversity within minorities results from differences in social history, individual life-history and current circumstances. To give one example, it is important to remember that there are very distinct differences in culture, background and experience between people migrating from different islands in the Caribbean; moreover, one cohort's experience of migration will be different from that of succeeding cohorts. Diversity within minorities is well-illustrated by the two important chapters which present the personal experience of, respectively, older Caribbean and Asian people, personal accounts which are an expression of social history as well as individual biography. In a society where nearly nine million people aged 65 and over are frequently referred to as if they are a uniformly homogeneous group with the same characteristics and needs, the variety and many differences to be found within the older population need to be emphasized again and again.

In pointing to features of the experience of older Afro-Caribbeans and Asians which are unique to individuals of a particular age and generation the authors are also illustrating a general truth about ageing: that one generation's experience of history and of old age will be different from succeeding generations. It is this changing experience of what it is to age as a member of a minority community which ensures that ethnicity, race and culture are not static entities: as Blakemore and Boneham observe in Chapter 5 on Afro-Caribbeans' experience, 'the meaning of being an older West Indian or

Afro-Caribbean person is dependent on the life course experienced and the historical period in which one is located'. The same can be said of older Asians and individuals from other minority groups.

Finally, this book should, I believe, make an important contribution to informing practice and the discussion of policy questions relevant to those working in the health and social services. Two chapters on, respectively, health, illness and health services; and on welfare and social services, aim to do this. The authors also include a very useful and possibly unique summary of 'options and insights for reflective practitioners' which fills a gap in the literature caused by the lack of discussion about the quality of relationships between black and Asian older people, carers and service providers.

Brian Gearing

References

Johnson, M. L. (1976) That was your life: a biographical approach to later life. In Munnichs, J. M. A. and Van Den Heuval, W. J. A. (eds), *Dependency or Interdependence in Old Age*. The Hague, Martinus Nijhoff.

Townsend, P. (1981) The structured dependency of the elderly: a creation of social policy in the twentieth century, *Ageing and Society*, 1, 5–28.

Walker A. (1981) Towards a political economy of old age, *Ageing and Society*, 1, 73–94.

Acknowledgements

We owe the deepest debts to Phil Nanton, University of Birmingham, who provided the initial stimulus and the original idea of a study of the needs of older black and Asian people in the English Midlands, and who has given encouragement throughout. Similarly, a great deal is owed to Anil Bhalla of the Asian Resource Centre, Handsworth, whose dogged persistence and hard work put the first major community survey of older black and Asian people on the map. Many other friends and colleagues have helped us, sometimes unwittingly, but we would particularly like to thank Harbans Maan (Margaret Boneham's co-worker from 1983 to 1985) who tirelessly translated interview material and clarified many aspects of family life in the Sikh community. Equally, thanks are extended to Meena Randhawa for her assistance in interviewing, reading draft material and for her wry sense of humour. Faith Elliott, of Coventry University, and Bill Bytheway, Julia Johnson and Mike Sullivan in Swansea all kindly tolerated requests to read draft chapters; though we alone are answerable for the final result, their comments and kind support were invaluable. In the final stages of writing, Brian Gearing of the Open University and Tony Warnes of the Age Concern Institute of Gerontology also provided much-needed encouragement. At a much earlier stage, the award of a research grant by the Nuffield Foundation to Ken Blakemore, to undertake a follow-up survey of older Asian and Afro-Caribbean people in Birmingham, is gratefully acknowledged. And we are indebted, in a different way, to both Margaret Barton in Liverpool and Eryl Evans in Swansea for their outstanding skills and patience in helping us prepare the manuscript.

We are especially grateful for the permission of the following to reproduce photographs in the book: Abdullah Badwi, John Reardon and the Dyche Collection, City of Birmingham Central Library.

Finally, in a league of their own, stand our respective spouses, Dilys and Roy, and our families. Without their continued support and positive attitude this book would not have been possible.

1

Introduction

Quietly and without much public attention, increasing numbers of Afro-Caribbean and Asian people are crossing their last significant frontier. They have already crossed other formidable frontiers: the frontier of immigration from a less industrialized to an industrial world, a racial frontier from a black or Asian to a predominantly white society, and a frontier of changing identity as they realized, in mid-life, that they have roots and commitments in a 'new' country as well as an old homeland.

Their last frontier, barring a return to the 'old' country, is the boundary which marks entry to old age. It is an ill-defined boundary, not always obvious even to those growing older, but the black and Asian people who came to Britain during the peak years of immigration, the 1950s and early 1960s, are either nearing or have reached retirement age.

The ageing of Britain's black and Asian older people has not been high on the agenda for either social research or for consideration by policy-makers in the health and social services. Reasons for this neglect are numerous, and are discussed more fully in the next chapter. They include such things as an underestimation of the significance to service providers of rising numbers of 'minority' older people in certain urban areas (pointed out, for example, by Ebrahim *et al.* 1991: 57); an association of race and ethnic relations with 'youth' problems such as unemployment and job discrimination, schooling, and urban disorder; and the slow development – in Britain and Europe if not in the USA – of multicultural perspectives in gerontological research. However, in a climate in which both public and private institutions are beginning to address the question of equal opportunity, the rights of older people and of people in minority ethnic groups are now less likely to be dismissed as fringe interests.

What significance does the 'last frontier' of old age have for Asian and Afro-Caribbean people and, by implication, for our general understanding of the ageing process? First, the process of growing old is far from uniform, and is in many ways a continuation of individual life patterns (Fennell *et al.* 1988: 51). Older people in minority communities illustrate the fundamental point that the so-called 'elderly' are not a faceless, anonymous category; they are a diverse and changing population of individual men, women, groups and communities.

Consideration of diversity helps us to explore the relative significance of physical, social and psychological ageing processes. Biographical and life-course perspectives in social gerontology (Johnson 1976) suggest that previous life experience may override the influences of common ageing processes on behaviour, attitudes and needs. Different experiences of migration illustrate this point. The contrasting life experiences of a refugee, as opposed to a long-settled 'economic' migrant or a recently arrived 'dependent' relative, will result in markedly different needs even though all three may be of the same age and of the same ethnic group.

Comparing people across two or more ethnic groups, we might ask whether the concept of an 'old age role' is meaningless, if experiences of ageing in different ethnic communities are so different. Or, against a background of cultural and other differences, whether it is possible to discern certain common aspects of ageing, or common needs and problems.

It should be clear from these opening paragraphs that our main concerns are twofold. First, we wish to address general comparative questions relating to both ageing and racial or ethnic relations. Second, we aim to help inform practice and to discuss policy questions of relevance to those working in health care, social and voluntary services. The beginnings of much of the interest in the position of older Afro-Caribbean and Asian people lie in community surveys which were primarily conducted to research need and to make policy recommendations (for example, Kippax 1978; Bhalla and Blakemore 1981).

However, older people in minority ethnic communities are of great significance in their own right. Their presence in a country such as Britain illustrates the role of ethnicity and culture in shaping everyone's later life. They point to a future of increasing ethnic diversity in old age, and to multicultural lifestyles and preferences among the older population. And, in the future, comparison between cohorts of 'native white', 'minority white' (for example, Irish, Polish) and 'minority black' or Asian people could give cross-cultural insights into the nature and impact of social and physical ageing.

Our book offers an overview of existing research, perhaps a 'base camp' before other studies begin to scale such peaks. In Chapter 2 we review previous community studies of older Asian and Afro-Caribbean people in Britain. The basic features of the main communities, in terms of numbers and minority status, geographical dispersal, age structure, gender and social class differences are outlined. We also discuss the constraints under which existing studies have been conducted. Much more work needs to be done, and there is a danger that after a burst of activity in the early and mid-1980s, research on 'minority ageing' in Britain will lose its momentum — a danger also noted by Rowland (1991) in Australia.

In Chapter 3 we briefly explore comparative perspectives on minority ageing, looking at the position of minority groups in several other countries. In order to make comparative observations it is necessary to draw upon important theoretical perspectives. These are chiefly variants of the modernization thesis, which proposes broadly similar trends towards nuclear family or small household living, and losses of social status and valued roles among older people. The value of this perspective is discussed in Chapter 3, together with other theoretical perspectives drawn from the field of race relations.

Continuing the overview in Chapter 4, we examine studies in the United States, Britain and elsewhere on the question of inequality, life chances and differences between the minorities and majority in old age. There is an argument about whether membership of a disadvantaged minority has a long-term negative effect on health and well-being, possibly shortening the lifespan or reducing the quality of later life. Set against this is the argument that minority ethnic identity is of positive value in protecting the individual from the harsh effects of social disadvantage or racial discrimination, and in nurturing ways of life which lead to contentment in old age.

The latter part of the book focuses on policy and practice implications, notably on health, illness and the health services (Chapter 7) and on welfare and social services (Chapter 8). However, as a bridge between discussion of the general position of older Asian and Afro-Caribbean people and of health and social needs, there are two chapters on the personal and group experiences of older Afro-Caribbean people (Chapter 5) and of older Asians (Chapter 6). In these chapters we have attempted to blend survey findings on perceptions of British society, neighbourhood, family and life satisfaction with the personal accounts given by older Asian and Afro-Caribbean people themselves.

The significance of race and ethnicity

As this book is concerned with the interrelationships between age, race and ethnicity, and with the experiences of older black and Asian people in particular, some preliminary explanation of this focus is required. Our prime aim is to throw light on the combined effects of race and age upon social status, health and welfare – hence the choice of 'black' minority groups rather than the 'white' minorities such as the Irish, Polish, Greek Cypriot or Jewish communities. The experiences and social position of older people in these latter communities are equally important and, as we mentioned, there is consider-able scope for comparative study of them.

Again, without denying the significance of their position in British society, we have not concentrated in this book on the history and experience of British-born older black and Asian people of the settled port communities such as Cardiff, Liverpool and east London. A main objective of our review of existing research has been to focus on the (mainly 1950s and 1960s) *migrant* experience of ageing in Britain. However, where appropriate (for example, in Chapter 3), we have made reference to the British-born older generation; their history has important implications for future cohorts of older black and Asian people.

Finally, we have not included in our coverage of Asian or black minorities the examples of Chinese, Vietnamese or other Southern or Eastern Asian communities, nor African communities which include small numbers of older people from Ghana, Nigeria, Sudan, Somalia and other countries. These groups also illustrate both the rich diversity of cultures in Britain and the as yet unfulfilled task of developing a fully comprehensive and comparative field of ethnic and cultural studies in gerontology: we concluded that more research needs to be done and specialized knowledge applied, before we could do justice to their case.

When we refer to 'black' and 'Asian' older people, therefore, the following main groupings are intended – though, as will become clear, even these are 'umbrella' terms which can mask important distinctions:

1 *Afro-Caribbeans*, sometimes termed 'African Caribbeans' (to denote their original African ancestry) or simply 'Caribbeans', are the people who migrated to Britain from the West Indies. The majority are from Jamaica, though other islanders are represented (see Chapter 5). The acquisition of a 'Caribbean' or 'black' identity is relatively recent, and older Afro-Caribbeans were brought up in societies in which island distinctions were of primary significance.

2 *Indian Punjabis* have migrated from the Indian state of Punjab. They speak 'Indian' forms of Punjabi (rather different from the Punjabi spoken across the border in Pakistan) and are almost entirely of the Sikh religion, though there are minorities of Hindus and Christians in Punjab state. To all intents and purposes, the older people referred to in this book are 'Punjabi Sikhs'.

3 *Indian Gujaratis* are people from Gujarat state, either from communities in the south of the state, around Bombay, or from northern Gujarat (Kutch). Their identity is marked mainly by the use of the Gujarati language (or the Gujarati dialect, Kutchi) and by adherence either to Hinduism (among the majority) or Islam.

4 *Pakistani Punjabis* come from the same broad geographical area as the Indian Punjabis – the 'land of five rivers' (Punjab) and they speak Punjabi. However, they will have come from the Pakistani side of the border, following Partition, and – apart from a tiny minority of Christians – are almost all Muslims (see Chapter 5).

5 *Pakistani Mirpuris* account for the majority of Pakistanis in Britain. They have come from the mountainous and agriculturally poor northern state of Mirpur, speak Mirpuri and are Muslims.

6 *Bangladeshis* are people who have mainly migrated from Sylhet, a northern interior district of Bangladesh, though a few have come from coastal areas. Bangladeshis in their childhood in 1947 lived in a country which was part of India (Bengal), but which after Partition became East Pakistan and eventually, following secession from Pakistan, Bangladesh. Bangladeshis speak their national language, Bengali, and those from Sylhet speak a dialect, Sylheti. All but a few Bangladeshis are Muslims.

7 *'East African' Asians* are people who have either migrated in the post-war period from India or Pakistan to East African countries (Uganda, Kenya, Tanzania, Zambia and Malawi) before coming to Britain, or are third- or fourth-generation descendants of Asians who migrated to Africa during an earlier stage of the colonial period. As a rule Asians in East African countries occupied an 'intermediate' social position between the former white elite (and their successors, the black political elite) and the majority of African

people. Many Asians from long-established East African families have never been to the Indian subcontinent. Most 'East African' Asians are Punjabis (either Sikhs or Muslims) and Gujaratis (a mixture of Hindus and Muslims).

Though the above seven groupings may be helpful in beginning to identify the older people who are the subject of this book, they are not all-inclusive. It is possible to come across middle-aged and older Indian or Pakistani people from any region or state, particularly those in 'middle-class' occupations from urban backgrounds. And there are always individuals or families who fit no broad category, such as the Sikh grandfather who has come to Britain not from Jullundur, Punjab, or from Mombasa in Kenya, but from Vancouver, Canada. Or there are the 'mixed marriage' families – unusual, but possibly having one grandparent from Gujarat and another from Punjab. Ethnic and cultural identity is often a complex matter, based not only on national and regional origin or upon religion, as the above groupings suggest, but on other sources too.

Defining race, ethnicity and culture

Older Afro-Caribbean and Asian people are seemingly different from the majority because they are 'black', or because they are in a minority 'ethnic' group. But what do these terms mean? The question of who belongs to which group, and the status attached to different groups, are matters of social convention – a fundamental point often made in the literature of race relations (for example, Rex 1986: 19). Distinctions of race and ethnicity are socially constructed.

The relative meanings of 'black' and 'white' are well illustrated by the Asians' position. Should Asians and people of Asian descent be called 'black'? Some insist that they should, because 'blackness' refers to status in a minority group disadvantaged by racial discrimination – that is, discrimination prompted by visible physical differences such as skin colour. Others, including a considerable number of Asians themselves, reject 'blackness' and maintain that their cultural identity and social position are more accurately defined by the umbrella term 'Asian'.

People of mixed descent or mixed race provide another example of the lack of hard-and-fast definitions of blackness. For example, an older 'black' person who has grown up in one of the long-established port communities in Cardiff or Liverpool may have had a 'white' mother and a 'black' father, with uncles and aunts of a dozen nationalities. Some would argue that whatever shade of skin that person had, mixed parentage often equates with being black, because experience suggests that he or she is likely to be treated as a member of a relatively powerless and disadvantaged minority. However, there could be a difference of opinion on this, because other aspects of one's background can override racial identity – for example, social class (working-class solidarity, or the middle-class background of a parent who was a teacher or religious minister), or other cultural ties (being a Liverpudlian or Welsh).

We do not wish to downplay the sharp significance of racial divisions and of discrimination. Racism dehumanizes and devalues individuals, whatever their achievements, to a common stereotype in the eyes of the prejudiced. But the point we wish to make is that, though often important, race is neither the sole element nor always the overriding aspect of identity.

This is an appropriate point at which to bring ethnicity into the discussion and to compare it with race. It is interesting to note that some commentators use the terms 'race' and 'ethnicity' interchangeably. This is especially the case among medical researchers (for example, Beevers 1981), who almost seem to view 'ethnic' as a 'polite' word for 'racial'. But in discussing 'ethnic differences in disease', such researchers are sometimes drawing attention to what they think are racial differences – for example, in heart disease rates between black and white people.

However, race and ethnicity are not synonymous and there is a case for making some firm distinctions. First, racial judgements are based on perceptions of physical appearance – skin colour, facial features, and so on – and these perceptions are in turn shaped by folk-myths and beliefs about the intrinsic, unchanging qualities or physical make-up of 'whites' and 'blacks'. Racism is therefore a kind of biological reductionism. For example, an older white person who sees an Afro-Caribbean coming to her church or day centre and does not want her there is expressing a racialist sentiment – a judgement which starts from an observation of skin colour and proceeds to elicit all sorts of stereotypes about 'black people'.

To describe older Asians and Afro-Caribbeans as members of 'ethnic minorities' does not therefore substitute for the term 'racial minority'. Seeing them as 'black' implies a general set of injustices, or a common social status which has emerged from the interaction between the white majority and the 'black' minorities.

But it is also possible to derive one's own identity, and to make judgements of others, on the basis of ethnicity. Just as everyone possesses a racial identity (black, white, or mixed parentage), so is everyone 'ethnic'. But what is ethnicity? Again, there is a range of definitions but broad agreement that one's ethnic identity is composed of *some*, if not all, of the following:

- ideas of 'peoplehood', or of one's own identity being bound up with a common past, a shared history of one's people. These feelings may be expressed in nationalism when the ethnic group is identified with a political unit or with political struggle (for example, the movement for an independent Sikh state, Khalistan). Ethnic identity is usually associated with a 'homeland' or land of origin. Individuals may grow up in the homeland, or perhaps in an overseas community or diaspora which continues to identify with the homeland (for example, Israel, Punjab).
- a language, either distinctive to the culture or shared with others (perhaps with distinctive dialects or other modifications).
- identification of the community with a particular religion (such as Sikhism) or with a world religion (such as Islam) in a way which fosters group allegiance.
- a distinctive culture. 'Culture' is itself an umbrella term referring broadly to a way of life: distinctive social institutions (family structures, marriage, initiation into the community), social norms, manners, attitudes and ways

of thinking, diet, dress. As Rowland (1991: 8) points out, culture and ethnicity are sometimes used interchangeably, but it is preferable to use ethnicity as the broader concept which includes culture, as well as the other components of ethnic identity.

As with race, defining one's own or others' ethnic identity is a subjective matter based on social conventions. The idea of perception is important. Wallman (1979: ix) suggests that 'ethnicity refers generally to the perception of group difference', meaning not objective differences but 'the *sense* of differences which can occur where members of a particular cultural . . . group interact with non-members'.

Over time, perceptions change. Saifullah Khan (1982: 209) writes: 'ethnic identity is not fixed, constant or single stranded; it is flexible and shifting on different levels according to situation and context'. This is an important point as far as ageing is concerned, because opinions vary as to whether ethnic loyalties fade with age, as older migrants adjust to their adopted country, or whether they are retained or even strengthened in later life.

Self-identification is therefore an essential element of ethnic identity. Just as people may be of mixed racial parentage, so may they have a mixed ancestry in ethnic terms. In such cases, deciding who one is, which language to speak, and so on, may be partly a matter of choice. Individuals themselves have ideas about who they are, or to what degree they are members of a community. Thus ethnicity need not only be a constraint, imposing upon people certain identities (for example, conformity to a particular religion, or to customs such as arranged marriage), but also a resource: a set of strategies for survival, for making sense of an unfamiliar world, and for drawing upon social support.

However, though ethnic identity may be a resource, it is also another way for 'outsiders' to make judgements about a group. These may be positive stereotypes (for example, the caring, extended Asian family) or terms of abuse. As Stone (1985: 35) reminds us, race and ethnicity are separate definitions of identity, but in practice may overlap. While white minorities such as Irish people in Britain have historically been the victims of cultural stereotyping (Jackson 1963), racialism as defined above is not involved. However, Asian and Afro-Caribbean people may be discriminated against on the basis of race *and* ethnicity. For example, a Pakistani family might be viewed negatively by white neighbours in racial terms and because of the way they perceive the family's foods, religion and ways of doing things.

In this respect there is no point in trying to make too many fine distinctions between racial and ethnic identity. Our argument, however, is that to concentrate only on race, or only on ethnicity, or to use the term ethnicity synonymously with race, neglects the specific impact of both factors on the identity of older Asians and Afro-Caribbeans. An emphasis on differences between ethnic groups can act as a divide-and-rule tactic to downplay or obscure the significance of race (Fenton 1986: viii). But attention to racism and discrimination does not mean that ethnicity should be left out of the picture. As Fenton (1986: viii) adds: 'In some contexts full attention to differences within broader groupings is necessary; island or country of origin loyalties or religious differences are real and important and other people's ignorance of them can be insulting'.

As we shall show, recognizing ethnic differences is vital to a thorough understanding of the lives of older black people: for example, in the patterning of gender and domestic roles, in health, and in social activities and expectations of old age (see Chapters 3, 5 and 6). But it is important to avoid an image of ethnicity which suggests a self-contained source of identity, or a property peculiar to ethnic minorities. In expressing ethnic preferences or distinct lifestyles, the minorities are not exhibiting peculiar traits: the white majorities also have ethnic and class cultural identities, whether they happen to be northern/southern English, Welsh, Scottish, or northern/southern Irish. There is no distinctive category of 'elderly ethnics', sometimes referred to in American gerontology.

In using both race and ethnicity as explanatory terms, therefore, it is important to consider the balance of power between the dominant and subordinate groups. A minority's racial and ethnic identity does not emerge in isolation, but from the interaction which takes place between minority and majority. The main question, which we will attempt to address in the remainder of the book, is how far this interaction between migrants and 'host' society is shaping the process of ageing.

2

Research, understanding and action

Thinking about ageing tends to be clouded by myths and stereotypes. This chapter is about such misunderstandings as they affect older black people. We will start by summarizing the major research findings, though more detailed discussion follows in the later chapters.

Our first object is to show that too little is understood of the needs and social position of older black people. A better understanding will be reached by beginning to question some of the generalizations and assumptions which have shaped current thinking. Our personal experience of conferences and seminars on the subject is that some misunderstandings are still quite common in the 'caring' professions: for example, the belief that many or most black migrants will return to live an old age in their countries of origin; the assumption that 'as there are not many older Asians or Afro-Caribbeans in my area' the needs of a minority are relatively unimportant; notions of 'extended families' in all Asian communities which invariably support their older people (or, conversely, a counter-myth which suggests that Asian families are breaking apart and that many older Asians are lonely and neglected); and, in similar vein, a view that all minority old people are hopeless victims of various forms of discrimination, people who are bound not to enjoy a happy old age in Britain.

Despite such misconceptions, it has often been argued at the same conferences and seminars that too much ink has been spilled on reports and surveys. Are older black people and their needs overresearched? Has research taken the place of, or priority over, action?

It is not easy to resolve these questions. There is an understandable impatience with social scientific research. Projects intended primarily to describe or analyse may not offer policy-relevant or prescriptive conclusions. And some have seen in research an exploitative element: that is, researchers who appear to suggest they are gathering data in order to stimulate official interest or action, but who are more concerned with their own careers or names.

But even if this argument is too cynical and individual researchers are working genuinely to improve awareness, there is a deeper worry: that 'doing a survey' might unintentionally sidetrack the need for change. So even if urgent problems or needs are exposed, the results of research may gather dust while those in the minority communities continue to wait for the potentially strong levers of research findings to be applied. In any case, as Bulmer (1986: 5) suggests, policy change rarely if ever results from the rational use of factual knowledge, though research is important in the way that it filters into the background knowledge or tacit assumptions of power-holders.

We believe, however, that it would be completely wrong to argue that there has been too much research of either the specific needs of older black or Asian people, or of the more general question of 'minority ageing'.

There is perhaps a case for asking whether we need any more of the same kinds of local community survey already conducted (see Table 2.1), mainly because these have successfully identified initial concerns and needs. But compared with the amount of public attention to, and research on, such questions as racial discrimination in housing, employment or education, the lack of research on the ageing of the black population is startling. If we are interested in a national picture of how older Asians, Afro-Caribbeans and other minority elders are faring, then research has hardly begun. Similarly, there has been almost no qualitative, in-depth research of white service providers (nurses, social service staff, and so on) and their social relations with older Asian or black users of services: what is it like to be an older Asian patient in a hospital ward, or to be in a minority of one or two in a residential home?

When the first community studies were carried out (Table 2.1) there was an almost complete lack of information. Thus the earlier studies played an important part in helping to initiate action (usually by voluntary groups) and in putting minority ageing on the agenda. As can be seen, all the research projects have been modest in scope and financed on a shoestring. Despite applications to major social research bodies such as the Economic and Social Research Council, no substantial resources have been granted. And there are certainly no grounds for the argument that lavish funding, for example from social service departments, has been diverted from practical action to research. In fact, the scarcity of adequate research funding has severely restricted the type and scope of study that could be carried out.

To date, most of the research has been based on door-to-door interview surveys. This may have been relatively easy to organize and it usually fits with service providers' views of what research should be: locate a 'target' population, ask some basic questions about their social circumstances and health, and discover their levels of knowledge of services as they exist now. Unfortunately, as with much survey-based research, there is a danger of ignoring what older people really want to say. Western assumptions about structured interviews may not be shared by respondents of minority cultures. Equally, basic assumptions about the services themselves – for example, the very idea of a mobile meals service whereby food is cooked and supplied by

Table 2.1 Examples* of community studies of middle-aged and older people in minority ethnic groups

Researchers/main publication	Place	Age and ethnic groups	Research methods
Nottingham SSD: Berry et al. (1981)	Nottingham	About to be, or over, pensionable age: 148 Afro-Caribbeans	Respondents traced through local Afro-Caribbean voluntary and religious groups
AFFOR: Bhalla and Blakemore (1981)	Birmingham	Pensionable age: 169 South Asians, 179 Afro-Caribbeans, 52 whites	Random sample questionnaire-based survey by professional research agency, plus interviews with service providers by Bhalla
Age Concern: Barker (1984)	London and Manchester	55 years and over: 619 people from West Africa, South Asia, West Indies	Random sample questionnaire survey
Greenwich SSD: Turnbull (1985)	London Borough of Greenwich	Pensionable age: 27 Afro-Caribbean and Asian people	Literature review and study of small sample (not randomly selected) chosen through personal contact and community groups
Department of Community Health, University of Leicester: Donaldson (1986)	Leicester	65 years and over (including women): 726 South Asians	Sample of elderly Asian patients drawn from family practitioner lists; some comparisons with local study of white patients
University of Bristol: Fenton (1986)	Bristol	'Middle aged' (45–60) and pensionable age: 98 Afro-Caribbeans, 104 South Asians, 52 whites	Sampling method not detailed: interviews restricted to four central wards in Bristol
Coventry City Council (1986)	Coventry	55 years and over: 71 Afro-Caribbeans, 1,163 Asians	Survey of approx. two-thirds of all black and Asian elderly people in Coventry: Asian respondents identified from Electoral Register and door-to-door visits, Afro-Caribbeans through community groups
Central Birmingham Health Authority: Cameron, Badger and Evers (1989)	Birmingham	66 disabled and frail older people (over retirement age): 35% black	Interviews with service providers of almost 500 randomly sampled elderly frail/infirm patients, and with 66 service users
Ebrahim et al. (1991)	North London	55 and over (mean age 62.9): 59 Gujaratis	Sample from general practice lists – response rate 88%. Asian respondents matched by age and sex with indigenous sample selected at random from GP lists

* With apologies to researchers not mentioned here – this is an illustrative list only

Appreciating diversity – a key step to understanding
Photograph: Abdullah Badwi

strangers – may not be explained; the older Asian or Afro-Caribbean is simply asked whether he or she has heard of the service.

In sum, most of the research has relied only on interviews with the 'client' groups and has been preoccupied with access to services. However, there has been little attention to the quality of services provided, or to what would be the most appropriate forms of service. Other neglected questions include inter-generational relationships in the various minority communities and the implications of changes in these for social support, or the danger of the abuse of older people. And moving away from matters of direct practical concern, it would be of great value to know more about the ageing process itself: how does racial and ethnic identity affect ageing or the meaning of old age? A longitudinal study – that is, following a sample of older people through time – would throw light on the ageing process and how needs might be changing.

However, the information we now have from various community studies does offer a large body of evidence. It has been collected piecemeal, but at least the diversity of studies has ensured that the research has not been dominated by a single group or organization. And we must not forget that, despite its limitations, the community study approach has had an important symbolic role. This should not be underestimated, because the ability of local groups to refer to their own studies has been vital in persuading those responsible for health and social services to begin at least to consider the needs of older black people.

Images of ageing in minority ethnic groups

The notion of an 'image' suggests an impressionistic view rather than a closely observed or scientific description. Anyone engaged in implementing policy or in delivering a service – a doctor, an occupational therapist, a district nurse or a social worker – works with images of different categories of patient or client. These have been found to influence strongly professional relationships and outcomes of treatment or intervention (see, for example, Rees 1978; Tuckett *et al.* 1985).

In discussions of the needs of older black and Asian people, three common images seem to recur: we have called these the *self-reliant pioneer*, the *gradually adjusting migrant* and the *passive victim* images. Each image is less of a description of reality and more of a stereotype. Primarily, such images tell us about practitioners' and commentators' *views* of ageing in minority ethnic groups. But though each image distorts, there is an element of truth in each. Someone who came to Britain in the early 1950s, who lived alone and in a self-sufficient way, could be regarded as a self-reliant pioneer. Nearing the end of his days, suffering from chronic illness, inadequate housing and not receiving adequate health care, he might now be seen as a victim of racial injustice. Yet, in having learned English and in now trying to surmount difficulties such as applying for additional social security benefits or making an appointment with a hospital consultant, he might also be seen as a gradually adjusting migrant.

The self-reliant pioneer

This is the image of migrants carrying to the host country their relatively unchanged ways of life. Each ethnic or religious group is seen as evolving its own way of coping with the demands of industrial society. The strength of the extended family in various Asian communities is a common element in the self-reliant pioneer image. It bears *some* resemblance to the truth, among Asians if not Afro-Caribbeans, in that typically it was the unattached younger males who migrated to Britain in the 1950s and 1960s – largely ahead of the women and children who, when they arrived, helped to settle and 're-ethnicize' Asian communities in Britain (Rose *et al.* 1969).

If personal problems raise their ugly heads, then this image encourages us to seek explanations based on 'poor adjustment'. Older black or Asian migrants may not speak English sufficiently well, they may be suffering from 'stresses of migration' or they may be considered deviant in some way by their own family or community. The following is an example of this form of explanation: elderly Asians' 'command of English is poor by comparison with the rest of the population . . . Few elderly Asians of either sex will have worked in Britain and . . . they may be at a severe disadvantage when referred for . . . care' (Mays 1983: 38).

There is some truth here about use of English, though not about lack of work experience among men and at least a significant minority of Asian women. But points of detail aside, such explanations as this can unwittingly distract attention from the failings of service providers (for example, a lack of translation services) and focus it on the apparent failings of individuals or minority cultures (Johnson 1984; Mares *et al.* 1985). Thus some pioneers 'fail'. Being different is seen as the reason for the problem.

In addition, the 'self-reliant pioneer' image perhaps gives too much weight to the traditional side of ethnic identity. The changes which have taken place since arrival in Britain – for example, in family relationships or in the aspirations and hopes of older people – can go unnoticed if the 'pioneers' are seen as people determined to live in traditional ways.

Change is evident in the gradual revision of hopes of return to live out one's days in the old country. As Anwar (1979: 222) concludes, for example, the myth of return is still prevalent among migrants from Pakistan, but over the years attitudes have become ambivalent. There is a distinction between myths or vague intentions and what older black people are actually deciding to do about returning. We will consider this in Chapter 5, but the survey carried out by Bhalla and Blakemore (1981) found that only 6 per cent of Afro-Caribbeans and 8 per cent of Asians were making, or had made, definite plans to leave the country; Barker's (1984) report showed that of a total of 619 black and Asian older people, only 5 per cent of men and 11 per cent of women had made specific plans to return to countries of origin. The proportions who said they intended to leave one day are much higher, pointing to the possibility of rising numbers of retired return migrants. If the majority of Afro-Caribbean and Asian older people *were* to act as 'traditional' self-reliant migrants have in Asia, Africa and the Caribbean, then a return to the home village or town at the end of one's working life would be quite likely. However, the evidence is uncertain and in many cases the ties to British life – chiefly children and grandchildren – have strengthened.

The gradually adjusting migrant

While 'self-reliant pioneers' are seen to be people who set their own priorities and find solutions to problems within their own communities, the image of the 'gradually adjusting migrant' suggests something different: it is a view which stresses the significance of integration. Older migrants, it is believed, will gradually lose the stronger elements of their cultural or ethnic identity. They will, in the case of non-English-speakers, learn English, adopt Western dress, adjust to norms of family life common in the majority, engage in leisure and educational pursuits in ways appropriate to their working- or middle-class position and, in old age, be prepared to use the social and health services common to all. This image is equivalent to the Westernization of old age, involving loss of status by older people and the transformation of families by modernizing influences (see Chapter 3).

Again, as with the self-reliant pioneer image, this contains a little truth. Most, if not all, older Asian and Afro-Caribbean people have had to make substantial adjustments in their way of life, attitudes and expectations since migrating to Britain. Clearly there are differences in this respect, as Barker (1984) suggests. A grandparent in his/her eighties migrating from India for the first time to join relatives in Britain could not be expected to make many adjustments easily, in comparison with say another eighty-year-old who has already made considerable personal adjustments after a working life in Britain.

But apart from these observations, there are flaws in the image of the gradually adjusting migrant. To begin with, there could be a strongly value-laden element: a hidden assumption that migrants to Britain *should* adapt and integrate. But what if the historical evidence suggests that many – and especially the older Afro-Caribbeans – tried to do this and were met with rejection and racism? (See Solomos 1989.) And even if we assume that racism has not blocked the path to adaptation or integration in every case, the notion that minorities should integrate at all levels (in housing, education and social life, as well as jobs) is a questionable one: it suggests that minorities' rights to retain distinctive ways of life, religious beliefs, and so on, are best given up, at most reluctantly tolerated. The image of 'gradual adjustment' therefore suggests not a pluralistic form of integration in which, within certain limits, all people are free to live as they wish, but a view of integration which actually means assimilation. It is perhaps this image more than any other which has had the most impact on the social welfare and health services, arising from historic welfare state assumptions that common services will be provided for all, and that individuals will adjust to these services (see Chapter 8).

The passive victim

Images of race relations and of Britain's black minorities change, as Connelly (1989) describes in relation to social services departments. Perhaps one of the more striking changes of attitude among 'caring' professionals in recent years has been the growing attention paid – officially, at least – to 'anti-racist' practice. Paternalistic, integrationist views have been challenged. Anti-discriminatory approaches to both delivering services and to monitoring their impact on minority groups have been stressed in health and social services training courses.

Though the full impact of these changes is still unknown, it is possible that they will have brought some benefit in at least challenging the complacency of earlier integrationist views. On the other hand, an approach which focuses solely on race and racism begins to obscure significant differences among black communities, and among older black people. These are not just cultural or ethnic differences, but also those of social class, employment, of age and period of migration, of locality and neighbourhood. And an insistence that racism is the key to understanding all the problems experienced by black people begins to create an unhelpful image of 'passive victims'.

While it is undeniable that racial discrimination and disadvantage are often the single most important set of influences on the lives of older black people, they have not affected all to the same degree or in the same ways; nor is racism the sole influence.

To argue that all are passive victims not only distorts the truth but is also condescending and undervalues their achievements and individuality. Little credit is given to those who have successfully struggled to overcome the inequalities with which they have been faced. In this sense the 'passive victim' image of older black people parallels one of the more general views of old age itself as one of helplessness and 'desolation' (Fennell *et al.* 1988: 8) in which the older person 'is depicted as an urban waif, lost in a concrete jungle she has never made'.

In sum, the 'passive victim' image may reinforce a view of older black and Asian people as an undifferentiated dependent group who need help and for whom things must be done. Furthermore, too great a preoccupation with racism might, if not applied carefully to practice improvements, lead to paralysis and disillusion among social workers, health service staff, and the like.

Inasmuch as these images do contain grains of truth, we argue that it is necessary to strike a balance between them rather than reject them altogether. The main point, perhaps, is to think self-critically about the images we hold and to apply them flexibly to given individuals or groups. It would certainly be wrong to plump for a single image or view, and there may be yet others to explore. With this in mind, we will now examine the major ingredients of our views of older black and Asian people – their minority status and the question of numbers; their age and its significance; and the role of gender and social class in forming their identity.

Image and reality

Minority status

A major reason for the non-appearance of older black people on the national agenda is their perceived status as a tiny minority within a minority. Put simply, it is easy to disregard a minority considered to be too small to bother about. For example, a government publication which appeared before most of the community surveys devoted nothing more than a paragraph to older people in minority ethnic communities. It suggested that 'the growth of this group will be slow' (Department of Health and Social Security 1978: 9) – a point challenged by the expectations of rapid increase as the main immigrant cohort reaches retirement age during the 1990s.

As Manuel (1982: 18) reminds us, however, 'the sociological understanding of a minority has nothing to do with the relative numbers of specific groups'. Understanding patterns of ageing among black and Asian people and their significance to society as a whole must go beyond arguments as to whether they form 1 per cent or 50 per cent of a given population or community.

It is also worth raising an ethical point about the supposed connection between the size of a group and the significance of its needs. Common sense tells us that the more people are in a given category of need – for example, homeless people or the disabled – the more attention such needs deserve. But while this is true, it could also be said that there are strong arguments for making special efforts to safeguard the rights or investigate the needs of relatively small groups. Just because 50,000, say, experience sharply felt needs it does not necessarily follow that their particular needs are less urgent or important than those of a group of 5 million.

Being an older person and a member of a minority ethnic community is not, of course, an indication of need in itself, and there is a danger of equating this with social problems. However, there is also the point that older black people in

Table 2.2 Ethnic groups by age in Great Britain

Racial/ethnic* group	Under 44		45–64 (men) 45–59 (women)		65+ (men) 60+ (women)		Total	
	Number ('000s)	%	Number ('000s)	%	Number ('000s)	%	Number ('000s)	%
Afro-Caribbean	346	72	109	23	27	6	482	100
Indian	623	80	124	16	32	4	779	100
Pakistani	379	88	48	11	6	1	433	100
Bangladeshi	95	86	14	13	2	2	111	100
Chinese	113	86	16	12	3	2	132	100
All above minorities	1,556	80	311	16	70	4	1,937	100
White	32,044	62	9,874	19	9,681	19	51,600	100

Source: Adapted from OPCS (1991: 25, Table 5.30)

* In the *Labour Force Survey*, 'respondents were asked to which ethnic group they considered they, and members of their houshold, belonged' (OPCS 1991: 24).

very small communities – for example, a few dozen older Afro-Caribbeans in a market town or 'shire' city – may experience problems and have special needs *because* they are in such a small minority and may be easily overlooked. Those living in provincial towns and cities face sharp problems of social isolation in old age unless a special effort is made to ensure that they have some access to friends and relatives, suitable shops and places of worship, as Boneham's (1987) work in Leamington Spa indicates.

Table 2.2 shows that, relative to the total population over retirement age and as a proportion of the minority ethnic groups themselves, the percentage of black and Asian older people is indeed a low one. Though the total will now be larger, in 1987–9 there were approximately 70,000. For a number of reasons, however, a view of this group as a small minority cannot be left at that. Rapid rates of increase, geographical clustering and questions about official statistics affect the picture.

Rates of increase will be rapid, especially over the next 20 years as the cohorts of migrants of the late 1950s and 1960s reach retirement age. Already the numbers crossing the frontier of 60 years of age represent the fastest-growing age group in the black community. The proportion of black and Asian people in the age group immediately before retirement (45–59/64) is substantial (16 per cent in 1987–9) and suggests a four- or fivefold increase among the pensionable age group by the year 2000.

These data refer to the proportions of older people in the black community as a whole – which includes a large number of younger people born in Britain. But leaving the British-born to one side, the ageing of the migrant generation is very noticeable. As early as 1981, for example, *over a third* of the Caribbean-born were aged between 45 and 59/64. Almost a third of the Indian-born were also concentrated in this pre-retirement age band, though Pakistani and Bangladeshi migrants tend to be younger, with only a fifth then aged 45–59/64 (OPCS 1983).

Table 2.3   Residence of minority ethnic populations by English region, Wales and Scotland (thousands)[1]

Region/Country	West Indian	Indian	Pakistani	Bangladeshi	Chinese	Minority ethnic population[2] as % of total population
Greater London	288	333	72	51	51	16.6
Rest of South- East	35	85	48	15	20	2.9
West Midlands	84	147	83	18	4	7.3
North West	25	57	75	5	12	3.6
Yorkshire and Humberside	24	44	87	6	8	4.2
East Midlands	16	88	15	3	7	4.0
South West	14	11	1	1	6	1.2
East Anglia	3	6	11	–	5	2.1
North	2	5	14	7	4	1.4
England	490.5	776.6	405.6	106.0	117.5	5.4
Wales	3.1	5.1	5.4	1.2	3.4	1.2
Scotland	0.9	4.8	17.0	0.9	4.1	0.9

Source: adapted from *Labour Force Survey* data summarized by Haskey (1991: 22,27)

[1] Figures for English regions have been rounded
[2] Additionally included African, Arab, 'mixed' and 'other'.

The concentration of older black people in certain regions and metropolitan areas (chiefly Greater London) also makes the label of 'small minority' rather misleading (see Table 2.3). As pointed out in a *Labour Force Survey* (OPCS 1991: 25), 'over two-thirds of the ethnic minority population live in metropolitan counties' and three-fifths of the Caribbean population, for example, live in Greater London. So while minority ethnic groups as a whole represent only approximately 5 per cent of the English population and form even lower proportions of the populations in Scotland and Wales, they constitute larger proportions in some, if not all, metropolitan districts. As Haskey (1991: 22) points out:

> the ethnic minority populations of the metropolitan county districts and London boroughs ... vary considerably as proportions of their total populations – the highest, 27 per cent, is estimated to be the London borough of Brent, and the lowest, 1 per cent, to be the Gateshead district of Tyne and Wear county.

In particular wards or inner-city areas, black and Asian people now comprise over half of the resident population. As the migrant generation ages, those over retirement age and particularly those in their fifties will become a substantial sub-group of these local majorities of black and Asian people.

Having said this, we should not forget the plight of the small numbers of older Asian and Afro-Caribbean people living outside the major cities, as mentioned above. Nor will an urban concentration of older black people ensure that all who wish for social support and company will get it. The Coventry (1986) survey, for example, showed a relatively dispersed pattern of residence among Afro-Caribbeans in the city. It appeared that some older black people lead quite isolated lives even though they are but two or three miles from social centres and other facilities.

Finally, there is a possibility that official statistics underestimate the totals of older black people, especially those who have come from India and Pakistan. Practitioners who have worked in community advice centres (for example, Sondhi 1985) suggest that not a few are unsure of their official 'British' age; Rack (1982: 85) makes the same point. Some may have initially understated their ages in order to secure employment. Consequently, official records and census returns may include a proportion who are actually older than stated. Indeed, it was striking to find that, in confidential interviews about age and year of arrival in Britain (see Chapter 6), the actual ages at which some Asian men had entered Britain were surprisingly high – in other words, they may well have felt they had strong reasons to disguise their ages.

Add to this the fact that for a variety of reasons 'estimates for ethnic minority groups are subject to relatively high sampling errors' (OPCS 1991) and there is certainly a case for keeping an open mind about the true ages of older Asian and Afro-Caribbean people. Unfortunately there is no reliable way of judging how extensive understatement of age has been. Sampling for the AFFOR (1981) survey in Birmingham suggested that numbers of older black and Asian people were significantly higher than the rate of increase expected from previous census totals. However, in the Coventry (1986) survey of selected city wards, which was of a 'census' type and aimed to contact all Asian households, there did not seem to be as great a discrepancy between the survey and the population census.

The significance of age

The image many have of older Asian and Afro-Caribbean people is that of a 'young old' group; broadly speaking, this is accurate. For example, in the Coventry (1986) survey, of the Asians and Afro-Caribbeans aged over 55, four-fifths were still under 70 years of age and two-thirds below 65. The Birmingham survey discovered similarly large proportions of people in their late fifties or early sixties (Bhalla and Blakemore 1981: 13). And as the people identified in these earlier surveys age into their seventies, they are being outnumbered even more by a much larger cohort coming into *their* early sixties – making minority older people a relatively 'young' group, as a whole, for the foreseeable future. This has considerable implications for the other images we discussed earlier, especially that of the 'passive victim'. For if most older black people are relatively young, and assuming they are not too badly affected by ill health and premature ageing, as a group they will be more likely than the 'older old' majority population to lead or play a part in their own community organizations, or to care for themselves without extra domiciliary help.

These are big 'ifs', however, and there are other serious points to consider. The first is that there *is* some evidence of poorer health, raising the possibility of premature ageing, among minority older people (see Chapters 4 and 7). This offsets somewhat the argument that rates of activity, self-care and good health will be higher among 'young old' Asians and Afro-Caribbeans than among the majority. A second point is that some respondents may have underestimated their true ages – the minority population may be older than it seems in community surveys as well as in census totals.

Third, the distinction between 'young old' and 'old old' is in itself a rather invidious one. Of course there are some unavoidable aspects of physical ageing and these should never be ignored. But the 'young/old old' distinction suggests that independence, activity and health are solely reflections of chronological age. Yet we know precious little about how the 'new' generation of majority white older people will take to life in their seventies and eighties, let alone what distinctions between 'young old' or 'old old' mean for people in minority cultures.

The significance of gender

It may be interesting to reflect on whether the notions of the 'self-reliant pioneer' or the 'gradually adjusting migrant', referred to earlier, suggest images of *male* migrants. If they do, this may reflect memories of earlier patterns of migration from the Indian subcontinent in which it was usual for men to arrive before women, though as far as Caribbean migrants were concerned the balance of the sexes had always been much more even than among Asians. However a common image of older migrants might still be that of male 'pioneers' and it might be assumed that older women remained a small minority in this group.

If so, such an image is becoming increasingly less representative, though of course in some Asian communities it is taking time for the balance of the sexes to become more even among older migrants. According to Shaw's (1988) report on population estimates, 55 per cent of the white population aged 45 and over is female, compared with 46 per cent of older people from India and only 35 per cent of those from Pakistan and Bangladesh. Thus the Pakistani and Bangladeshi communities are rather different from the other communities. The larger proportion of males in the Bangladeshi community is partly a reflection of relatively recent entry to the United Kingdom: a third came between 1980 and 1984, and 15 per cent between 1985 and 1986 (OPCS 1991: 27).

This would not apply as much to older Pakistanis, who form a longer-established community. However, both the Bangladeshi and Pakistani communities are strongly Islamic. It is likely that for a variety of traditional and religious reasons Muslim women have not been encouraged to migrate and settle in the West as often as the women of the other Asian cultures.

But, more generally, it is important to remember that the above comparisons are based on the middle-aged as well as older people in different ethnic groups. However, shorter life expectancy among males tends to reduce male predominance in minority ethnic groups in the pensionable age group. Table 2.4 shows that as long ago as 1981 two-thirds of older (pensionable age) people in the Caribbean, Indian and 'East African' communities were women, matching

Table 2.4 Percentages of females among those born in Caribbean, Asian and East African countries, resident in the UK, 1981

Country or region of birth	Percentage female in 45 years to pensionable age group	Percentage female in pensionable age group	Total of women aged over 45
Caribbean	42	65	52,800
India	41	65	71,176
Bangladesh	14	37	1,553
Pakistan	32	57	13,593
East Africa	45	68	7,660
All New Commonwealth* and Pakistan	40	64	182,389
UK	44	67	10,329,811

Source: OPCS (1983: Table 2) (adapted from pages 58–59)

* Includes other New Commonwealth countries than those mentioned above.

almost exactly the proportion of women in the population as a whole; by then the Pakistani community had a majority of women in its older migrant generation, albeit a lower percentage, and only among Bangladeshis were older women in a minority.

And what of the three images of older black people we identified earlier? We suggest that older Asian women are much more likely to be seen as 'passive victims' than as either 'self-reliant pioneers' or 'gradually adjusting migrants' (see, for example, Wilson 1978, for a portrayal of Asian women as victims). But is this fair? It seems important to try to jettison stereotypes and to reconsider how a variety of domestic and work roles have affected older minority women (Allen 1982). In later chapters (5 and 6) we will do this, and consider how social change has affected older men as distinct from women.

The significance of social class

Black and Asian people of all ages are more likely to be of manual or 'working-class' occupational background than the white majority (see Table 2.5). As the *Labour Force Survey* shows, for example, over 70 per cent of Afro-Caribbeans are in manual jobs compared with 54 per cent of white (OPCS 1991: 28). For Asian people in work, however – and this discounts many Asian women – class differences are rather uneven. Among Indians, there is no racial disparity in the sense that an equal proportion to whites are in manual jobs (54 per cent). However, Pakistanis and Bangladeshis are as likely as Afro-Caribbeans to be manual workers.

The data in Table 2.5 present only one view of social class, and take no account of such problems as racial discrimination at the workplace (for example, in terms of promotion or rates of pay). There is also a higher risk of unemployment among black communities (Brown 1984).

Table 2.5   Afro-Caribbean, Asian and white people aged 16 and over, by socio-economic group (percentages) and unemployment, 1987–89

Socio-economic group	Afro-Caribbean		Indian		Pakistani and Bangladeshi		White	
	Men	Women	Men	Women	Men	Women[1]	Men	Women
Professional	3	1	11	4	5	–	7	2
Employers/managers	8	6	19	7	16	–	20	10
Other non-manual	17	54	16	45	11	–	18	52
Skilled manual	43	5	35	14	32	–	37	8
Semi-skilled manual	21	24	16	27	31	–	13	21
Unskilled manual	7	9	3	3	6	–	4	7
Armed forces/ inadequately described/not stated	1	0	0	0	0	–	1	0
Total	100	100	100	100	100	–	100	100
N ('000s)	117	115	194	128	88	22	13,702	10,238
Unemployed (%)[2]	18	14	10	13	25	–	9	8

Source: OPCS (1991: 26,28)

[1] Data on Pakistani and Bangladeshi women not provided by the *Labour Force Survey*.
[2] OPCS (1991: 26, Table 5.33) lists unemployed between 1987 and 1989 as a percentage of the economically active.

The information gives a background to social class in Asian and Afro-Caribbean communities, but in what ways, if at all, are social class categories applicable to the older people in the communities? Tables 2.6 and 2.7 present the findings of two of the community surveys, and they give a rather different picture from the socio-economic backgrounds of younger black and Asian people.

Hardly any older Asian or Afro-Caribbean people had worked in non-manual jobs before retirement: neither in professional or managerial occupations nor in clerical or 'lower middle-class' jobs. There is a geographical effect to consider here, in that the West Midlands samples shown in Tables 2.6 and 2.7 include larger numbers of factory workers and other manual workers than are found in communities in the East Midlands, or in London and South East England. This geographical distinction applies especially to the Indian community; in Birmingham and Coventry, large proportions of older Indian men are Sikhs who have worked in the car industry or in other engineering industries, whereas the London and Leicestershire communities of Indians include most of those with professional, managerial or business backgrounds. It can be misleading to discuss the 'social class' of older black and Asian people without some reference to region and ethnicity.

However, many older Asian and Afro-Caribbeans nearing retirement settled for manual jobs despite the fact that some – especially the Afro-Caribbeans – had educational qualifications which merited employment in non-manual work or other manual jobs with higher pay. While racial discrimination and high unemployment continue to depress employment prospects among

Table 2.6 Occupational class of older Asian and Afro-Caribbean people in Birmingham (percentages)

Occupation*	Asians		Afro-Caribbeans	
	Males	*Females*	*Males*	*Females*
Professional	7	0	1	0
Semi-professional	5	0	3	0
Skilled manual	19	2	16	7
Semi-skilled	13	0	24	25
Unskilled	50	8	56	55
Never in paid work	6	89	0	13
No answer	0	2	0	0
Total	100	100	100	100
N	107	62	68	111

Source: unpublished data from the AFFOR survey (Bhalla and Blakemore 1981)

* Defined according to last occupation before retirement and by categories used by MAFS (Market Research) Ltd.

Table 2.7 Occupational class of older[1] Asian and Afro-Caribbean people in Coventry (percentages)

Occupation/Social class[2]	Asians	Afro-Caribbeans
I	0	0
II	1	1
III (Non-Manual)	1	2
III (Manual)	14	28
IV	8	8
V	17	46
Housewife/never in paid work	45	9
No reply, not classified	14	6
Total	100	100
N	1,122	112

Source: unpublished data, Coventry (1986)

[1] Aged 55 and over.
[2] According to Registrar General (census) categories.

younger black and Asian people, the older generation is a more solidly 'working-class' group, at least in areas like the West Midlands and the industrial North of England, with fewer of their number in non-manual and supervisory posts than younger workers.

Working-class identity is particularly strong among certain communities and sub-groups of workers. For example, some older Indian manual workers in the West Midlands and in other areas have strong memories of, and loyalties to, the pioneering union activities of the Indian Workers' Association. From time to time Asian women workers have been swept up in union disputes with 'sweatshop' employers, and some of these women are now nearing retirement age. Similarly, and despite sometimes being kept at arm's length by white trade unionists, older Afro-Caribbean workers have played an important part in the public sector unions. However, a high proportion of Asian women have never been in paid employment and, never having been unionized or involved with the social side of work life, do not identify with an occupational or social class community.

In retirement older black people tend not to be as well-off as the average white older person of working-class background, but there is a small minority of older black people who are relatively better-off and who have a 'middle-class' professional, managerial or business background. Castles and Kosack (1985) argued that immigrant workers in Western Europe have been disproportionately located in the less desired spheres of employment, forming a lower stratum or 'underclass'. The evidence presented in Table 2.5, on the minority population as a whole, does not support this contention: though black workers are found disproportionately in manual occupations, the proportions in *skilled* jobs are relatively high.

Westergaard and Resler (1977) made the same point by reference to earlier data on the distribution of New Commonwealth migrants in the British labour force. A significant number of those now nearing retirement first found work in skilled jobs, though the distribution of black workers as a whole was skewed towards the less skilled and less well-paid jobs. In 1966 the proportion of West Indian men in unskilled and semi-skilled work was less than half (about the same as among migrants from Ireland). Among Asian communities, only migrants from Pakistan had a majority in unskilled or semi-skilled work (1977: 357).

As Westergaard and Resler admit, however, the proportions of women from the Caribbean or Asian countries in non-manual or skilled manual work were not as high as among black and Asian men. We must also take into account the impact of redundancies, unemployment and other causes of downward mobility which may have depressed the class positions of workers sampled in 1966. Therefore the Castles and Kosack thesis is partially borne out by the class position of older migrant black and Asian people, or at least those interviewed in the Midlands (Tables 2.6 and 2.7), many more of whom have been employed in unskilled or semi-skilled jobs than younger or middle-aged black people.

In comparison to general working-class standards, considerable numbers of older black people are economically disadvantaged. Their migrant background can compound the economic inequalities of the working life. As the state pension scheme works on the insurance principle, some find they have not had time to build a complete record of contributions to qualify for a full pension. And older Asians, a majority of whom have worked in the private sector, sometimes find that employers have evaded contributions to their pensions, again jeopardizing their pension rights. Though it is possible to claim additional state benefits to bring income up to a minimum level, these are means-tested and not always taken up. The reasons for this and its impact on income levels will be more fully discussed in Chapters 4 and 8, but the point to note here is that the welfare system is often far from a levelling influence on income in old age.

Those who have never been in paid work are even more likely to be poor.

This category includes a majority of, but not all, the Asian women, a small proportion of Afro-Caribbean women, and older so-called 'dependent' people who arrive as retired workers. The appropriateness of social class categories is rather questionable in these cases: are they 'working-class', and does this label mean anything to people who have never been in paid employment or a trade union?

Some older people – Asians from East Africa in particular – entered Britain as refugees rather than as voluntary or economic migrants. Most refugees found work, many in manual or 'working-class' jobs. But as a significant proportion of Asian refugees are well-educated and some formerly had jobs in business or public administration, a view of them as 'working-class' would not accurately depict how they see themselves and could mask the downward social mobility some have experienced.

Finally, the small but significant group of older black and Asian people who have a socio-economic position appreciably *above* the majority of retired working-class people in inner-city areas should not be forgotten. The AFFOR (1981) survey showed that, while only 4 per cent of older whites had a weekly income above the average in the area, 9 per cent of older Afro-Caribbeans and 15 per cent of Asians reported these higher incomes.

There is not yet a sizeable 'middle-income' group of older people in all British Asian and Caribbean communities (though such communities do exist in Leicester, London and elsewhere). Older black people who have become relatively better off are not necessarily *much* better off. However, the development of 'middle-class' lifestyles among older Asian or Afro-Caribbean people, such as a desire to live in suburban areas, should not be ruled out, and small proportions of the middle-aged are already changing in these ways (see Chapter 6).

White people with average or above-average incomes have been leaving inner-city neighbourhoods in increasing numbers – the phenomenon of 'white flight'. However, the small number of better-off older Asians and Afro-Caribbeans have, in the main, stayed. Their presence will undoubtedly be more significant than their numbers suggest, not only as individual examples of success, but also as a potentially influential pressure group to support voluntary social services and other initiatives. Whether or not the images of the 'self-reliant pioneer' or 'gradually adjusting migrant' throw much light on their role, they are certainly not 'passive victims'.

To summarize, class is perhaps a term best used as a starting point than as a final statement about the social position of older black people. Many are aptly described as belonging to one or another level of the 'working class', but the existence of sharp deprivation, on the one hand, and a small but growing number with non-manual and skilled occupational backgrounds, on the other, complicates the picture.

Conclusion

Given the rather bewildering variety of personal and cultural backgrounds among the older 'black' population, it is understandable that many who have thought about the question of minority needs have looked for common themes and images. Indeed, there are some valid generalizations, as we showed: the majority of older Asians and Afro-Caribbeans are 'young old' people; two-thirds are women; they are more likely than older whites to have had manual or 'working-class' jobs; they are a 'minority in a minority'; and they share common experiences of being discriminated against, on grounds of both race and ethnic identity.

However, we attempted to show how each of these generalizations can seriously mislead if unthinkingly applied to important sub-groups of older black people. Understanding racial oppression is not the single key to an understanding of ageing in the Afro-Caribbean and Asian communities (though it may be an important one). Not all of these older people are in poverty or dependant on outside help; neither, as is sometimes supposed, have they all 'gradually adjusted' to life in Britain or remained, like 'self-reliant' pioneers, within enclosed families and communities.

At the end of this chapter we therefore hope to have questioned some of the preconceptions or assumptions about the position of older Afro-Caribbean and Asian people in British society which we mentioned at the beginning. At the same time, we hope that other, clearer images have begun to take shape.

3

Comparative perspectives

The purpose of this chapter is to set the experience of Britain's older black and Asian people in a comparative context. Every minority's experience is unique, but not without parallels elsewhere. There are examples of 'minority ageing' across the world, from the Welsh in Argentina and Italian Americans in the USA to mixed-descent 'Anglo-Indians' in India and Vietnamese people in Australia.

However, our aim is not to provide an exhaustive list of comparisons. Comparative gerontology can offer fascinating overviews of minority ageing (see, for example, Gelfand and Kutzik 1979; Cowgill 1986; Driedger and Chappell 1987; Markides and Mindel 1987), but we shall be selective and ask what light examples of minority ageing can throw on the fortunes of Asian and black people in Britain.

Drawing on comparative insights, we suggest that two sets of factors will shape the ageing of black and Asian people in Britain. The first is their own expectations of old age and the status of older people in their former countries. Childhood socialization and memories of their parents and grandparents will deeply affect what older black and Asian people expect of others and of themselves. Over time, continuity may be threatened by social change among the second, third and fourth generations: does comparative evidence suggest that minority ethnic identity is inevitably eroded over time?

The second factor is the relationship between the minority community and the majority. How far the community is seen by the majority as either accepted and permanent, or 'migrant' and temporary, and how people in the minority *themselves* view their position, will have an impact on the older members of the minorities. Being forced, or wishing, to maintain a distinctive ethnic and racial identity will have consequences for the strength of ethnic influences on old age.

Old age, tradition and modernization

Are older migrants from the less industrialized to the industrialized world carriers of 'traditional' patterns of ageing? Would it be helpful to see older Asians and Afro-Caribbeans in Britain as people who are cushioned by traditional attitudes towards older people – respect, ideas of familial duty to the aged, and so on – or at least as people who are struggling to regain the traditional status accorded to the aged in their former homelands?

Though such images strike a chord, there are major doubts about the validity of notions of 'traditional' and 'modern' patterns of ageing. The 'tradition to modernity' view of ageing, as advanced initially by Cowgill and Holmes (1972) and subsequently revised (Cowgill 1974) has been heavily criticized from many quarters (for example, Laslett 1976; Dowd 1980; Palmore and Maeda 1985). In fact criticizing modernization theory has almost become a folkloric tradition in its own right. With any global theory there are bound to be contradictions and inconsistencies, but we suggest that the perspective should not be entirely rejected.

The evidence on changing patterns of ageing across the world, brought together by Cowgill and Holmes (1972), identified four main modernizing influences which tend to devalue the status of older people: improvements in health, especially in youth and middle age, which have increased longevity and the proportions of dependent older people in the population; migration and urbanization, leading to the break-up of the extended family as a domestic unit in which the elders used to play a dominant role; the application of science and technology, which renders redundant formerly treasured skills guarded by the older and more experienced; and the rise of mass education, which supposedly invalidates tradition.

One flaw in this model is that it may foster a myth of unconditional reverence for old age in pre-industrial or traditional societies. However, variations in social organization are vital in determining the status of older people. There is no such thing as a common traditional 'elder' role. In reviewing a range of anthropological studies, Victor (1987) concludes that there is no clear association between the status of older people and the level or type of economic development: among nomadic societies, for example, are those which were very protective of the old and others which were the opposite. Simmons (1945: 243) also concluded that there was enormous variety among preliterate societies in attitudes towards old age, 'varying from the height of homage to the depths of degradation'.

Simmons made the point that, as a rule, respect for older people was based on an asset which they had such as skills and knowledge, magical powers or the ability to tell stories. Reid's (1985) study of status among older Australian Aboriginal people demonstrates that, though Aborigines have a reputation for treating all older people with respect and affection, 'the actual situation of an old person depends on an interplay of . . . factors, including personal qualities, family support, seniority, sex, ecology and land use patterns and the effects of white colonisation and social change' (1985: 69).

This is also the case in 'traditional' Jamaica, according to Foner (1979). She suggests that older people in the West Indies might be treated with more

Home for these ex-seamen from Somalia is now Toxteth, Liverpool
Photograph: Abdullah Badwi

courtesy than in England, but beyond this one's standing in the rural community is dependent upon either inherited status (land, family, class and racial identity) or achievements (capital, property, educational qualifications, political office); old age alone cannot elevate one's status.

Similarly, Harlan's (1964) study of three village communities in India, designed specifically to test modernization theory, found that respect for older people was conditional – even in the most 'traditional' community. Income and education had much more significant effects on prestige than age *per se*. His study is particularly revealing because it attempted to look beneath the surface politenesses of family life. Though superficial observation of interactions between grandparents and their younger relatives suggests unconditional deference and respect for the old, and signs of pleasure and friendliness towards older relatives, Harlan found that the old would be (politely) reminded of the limits of the respect to be accorded to them.

Thus the potentially vulnerable position of older people in many Indian societies has its roots in the past, and is not necessarily linked with recent processes of modernization. Also, Harlan's findings suggest that the presence of nuclear families among Indian and other Asian communities in Britain (see Chapter 5) is not necessarily a sign of 'corrosive' or modernizing change, because the extended family (as a domestic unit) neither is a universal form of family in India nor has uniformly protective functions as far as older people are concerned.

Similarly, but with reference to ethnic minorities in Australia, Rowland (1991: 11) suggests that

> the Cowgill hypothesis is likely to be a misleading source of expectations . . . because it assumes that . . . the process of modernisation has brought a shift from extended to nuclear family living. Contrary to popular opinion, extended family living was not part of the experience of the majority of settlers . . . though some Southern European groups are exceptions.

Despite all these arguments, some would still maintain that modernization theory has value in understanding the kind of changes older Asian and Afro-Caribbean people are going through. Cowgill (1986) and, in rather more injured tones, Holmes (1987) have stoutly defended their approach. In response to the criticism that modernization theory assumes uniform outcomes and a unilinear process of change from 'tradition' to 'modernity', Cowgill (1986: 186) argues that 'modernization . . . will never proceed in a uniform pattern; there will always be lags and leads, starts and stops, perhaps even reversals'. Equally, the idea of universally high status among the old in traditional society is rejected as an oversimplification and distortion of the theory: 'in all societies we find much diversity among the elderly. Their status and financial security always vary by gender . . . there are also differences . . . by social class in nearly all societies' (1986: 178).

The authors are therefore ready to concede that, in a culturally diverse world, communities modernize in their own ways. Some support for their view is found in signs of loss of status and of isolation or disengagement among the old in traditionally 'age-honouring' societies – those often held up as examples to refute the theory of modernization: for example, Japan (Holmes 1987) and certain African societies (Peil 1985, 1987; Tout 1989).

However, although the modernization perspective may have some attractions, problems seem to arise when it is applied to particular cases. One is drawn back to explaining how given migrant communities change, but to describe each and every adaptation as a variation on the theme of modernization may be misleading.

Differences in patterns of ageing among other former migrant communities illustrate this point. Srivastava's (1974) history of the Sikh community in Vancouver, Canada, shows that nuclear families are now the norm and that older people not infrequently live alone, or in couples. But this does not necessarily mean that such change is entirely a result of modernization. Another interpretation is that earlier Sikh migrations to western Canada were met with intense racial hostility from the white Canadian population (including threats to deport the entire community). Indian Sikhs were at best barely tolerated and were expected to conform to prevailing norms, which discouraged living in larger family groups. Yet these Canadian Sikhs retain links with their families and community in India and elsewhere, and continue to subscribe to Sikh values even though their residence patterns have been changed fundamentally.

Notions of modernization may therefore be misleading when distinctive ethnicity is equated with the 'traditional' end of a tradition-to-modernity spectrum. Some ethnic or cultural groups seem to prize extended family living, or modified versions of it, and support 'traditional' views of the role of older people – but others do not. C. L. Johnson's (1986) study of the high status of older people in an Italian American community demonstrates that 'while it is clear that individuals have some latitude in how they conform to traditional European *mores*, the force of culture is seen as pervasive and prescriptive even after three generations' (Holmes 1987: 197).

Referring to a more recent migrant group, a Corsican community in Paris, Cool (1981) concludes that older people in this community enjoy a relatively high degree of respect and authority because they have certain resources. These migrants had come from a pastoral economy, following established chains of contacts, to find work and a better standard of living in Paris. The pattern is similar to the migration of Punjabi Sikhs or of migration from the Caribbean to Britain. Older Corsicans have successfully established the interpersonal networks which give younger migrants access to jobs and accommodation. They also occupy valued roles as guardians of Corsican culture and representatives of the Corsican community.

Neither example completely invalidates the modernization thesis: in fact, they lend some support to notions of 'traditional' culture and, according to Rosenthal (1983), such studies contain a 'disguised' form of the modernization thesis. Arguably, such cases represent the examples of 'lag' or diversity to which Cowgill (1986) referred. But they also raise questions about the advisability of trying to squeeze a wide variety of examples of change into a 'tradition-to-modernity' framework – a task rather like driving a large truck into a narrow cul-de-sac. Modernization theory may be useful as a 'sounding board' (if only to show what is *not* happening to the status of older people), but may often obscure more than it reveals about ageing and social change in minority ethnic communities.

Minorities and majorities

Comparative study suggests that the experience of being an ageing migrant will be very much affected by the way one's community has been accommodated in the majority society or 'body politic'. A white English person growing old in Canada, for example, will perhaps experience relatively few cultural disjunctures or feelings of difference (unless he or she moves to Quebec). Though the present generation of English migrants in Canada are a minority, they are almost indivisibly part of the dominant culture and a long tradition of British colonization which has shaped Canada itself. But consider the contrasting historical experience of other Canadian minorities: native Canadians, the Sikh community mentioned above, or the French-speaking community.

The size of a minority is a consideration even though, as we said in Chapter 2, not too much significance should be attached to numerical strength. For one thing, as van Amersfoort (1982) reminds us, numbers matter in parliamentary political systems. Where minorities are large, the 'ethnic vote' can be mobilized to press for minority recognition or for national resources.

Thus the experience of growing old in 'immigrant societies' such as the United States, Canada and Australia differs in significant ways from ageing in countries with a much smaller minority population such as Britain. Glazer and Moynihan (1975: 15) refer to the development of ethnicity as an 'organizing principle' in some heterogeneous or plural societies, though this may conflict with other principles of government and representation. Where the state recognizes the legitimacy of ethnic groups or blocs for purposes of distributing welfare or mobilizing public opinion, this could have beneficial implications for minorities, or for 'minorities in minorities' such as older people.

In the USA African Americans of all ages comprise 15 per cent of the total population, and then other communities form additional substantial minority groups. The importance of the minority old is revealed by the fact that they number about 9 million and account for almost two-fifths of all American older people (Markides and Mindel 1987). In Australia older migrants from non-English-speaking countries will comprise over 60 per cent of all overseas-born older people, and almost a quarter of all older Australians, by the year 2000 (Rowland 1991: 17).

Despite the persistence of some minority disadvantage (for Australian examples, see Rowland 1991: 43), growing older amidst a sizeable community has a different 'feel' from that of being in a minority of a few per cent or less, as in Britain. Confidence among the minorities about their identity is likely to be higher. People in positions of intermediate authority and service providers or 'gatekeepers' are much more likely to be drawn from the minorities. In some American cities, for example, almost entire police departments, the postal service and other public institutions are run by African Americans. Access to suitable or ethnically specialized community services and health practitioners is likely to be much easier, though this is not the case in Australia, where wider geographical dispersal of the minorities works against community provision of ethnic-specific services (Rowland 1991: 19).

The questions of whether one grows old in an 'immigrant' society such as Australia, or in a small or large minority, are not the whole story. As van Amersfoort (1982) suggests, a minority's *status*, its level of social influence and power, are also affected by its historical relationship with the majority. This is illustrated by the oppressed position of indigenous or native minorities – for example in Canada, the USA and Australia. In all three countries these minorities were faced with near-extermination as a result of white coloniz-ation: the combined effects of war, being driven into reservations, the introduction of diseases and alcohol, and cultural suppression (Stone 1985: 144). Later policies towards indigenous minorities in the USA and elsewhere have veered between assimilationism, or forced integration, and attempts to 'protect' ethnic minorities by segregation, as if they were relics in a cultural theme park.

Black and Asian migrants to Britain came from societies which had also been deeply affected by white colonialism. In the case of slavery in the Caribbean, this again included attempts to eradicate ethnic identities by suppression of African languages and cultures. British colonization of the Indian subcontinent took a different form and relied mainly on 'indirect rule' through Indian states. So while it also buttressed European myths of racial and cultural superiority, the historical effect is that modern stereotypes of South Asian minorities and of Afro-Caribbeans differ: it has been shown that British teachers, for example, find it hard to acknowledge the existence of distinctive Caribbean cultures (Rampton 1981), whereas Asian cultures are seen as 'too distinctive' or alien.

Another point of difference between the migrant and indigenous minority is that the latter is a conquered and often demoralized people, whereas most in the former (except for refugees) are economic migrants or dependants who choose to live in a new country. However, as Stone (1985: 53) points out, oversimplified distinctions between migrant and indigenous minorities 'raise a number of basic questions, not the least of which is how to define an "indigenous" population'.

Former migrant groups may become 'indigenous' over time. Britain, for example, has a history – stretching back to the eighteenth century and beyond – of settlement by substantial numbers of black people (Fryer 1984). Many of these migrants settled with indigenous people and their descendants were assimilated. But there are also seaport communities of black, Asian and other people, dating in the main from the nineteenth century (Little 1947: 56), which have maintained ethnic and racial distinctiveness. These may be regarded as 'indigenous' in two senses: first, because many in such communi-ties have grandparents or even great-grandparents who were born in the same place; and second, because intensely local feelings of identity have formed, transcending if not replacing the diverse ethnic and national origins of their inhabitants. Butetown in Cardiff is a good example, though similar local communities exist in Liverpool, London docklands and in ports in other countries – San Francisco, for example.

The social and policy implications of these 'enclave' minority communities go far beyond their boundaries. Integrationist thinking suggests that the needs of older black and Asian people and the problems they face will gradually disappear in a process of adjustment. But the history of established or indigenous minority communities gives a different picture: a story of continuing racial conflict and economic disadvantage, of 'defended' communities which have maintained cultural traditions, religious affiliations and support systems, and of neglect by officialdom evidenced – until recently – by the non-provision of ethnically sensitive social services and a lack of representation in the employment structures of local service providers.

Little's (1947) history of Butetown shows that racism has always been a problem and has often served as a focus for local competition over jobs and housing. On 10 June 1919 there were serious outbreaks of violence in which whites attacked Butetown residents, killing one person and injuring many others; they also damaged property and burned down lodging houses. There were similar race riots involving murder in other ports, notably Liverpool (May and Cohen 1974).

During the 1920s black seamen and other residents suffered racial harassment from local police forces (Little 1947: 65) who applied restrictions and deportations under the Aliens Order legislation of 1920 and 1925 punitively, indiscriminately and without proper regard to citizenship or nationality rights.

The post-war history of Butetown and similar communities in other ports is one of attempted 'redevelopment'. In Butetown's case, the unique strengths of the local community were noted at the time (Roberts 1957) but redevelopment was done in ways which destroyed many community supports: for example, by building multi-storey blocks of flats and new street patterns, and by trying to disperse local families in council accommodation throughout the city.

In sum, the attitude of the white majority towards the small indigenous black, Asian and Arab communities has always been one of rejection and victimization. Until recently, it has proved difficult to achieve any recognition by the authorites of special needs among older people in these communities, though in the past ten years in Liverpool, for example, several important voluntary initiatives have been established: for instance, group homes for older Somali, Chinese, Nigerian and Caribbean people (Liverpool Personal Service Society 1988) and a day/community centre for older Chinese people (Chiu 1989).

The history of the indigenous seaport communities therefore provides a salutary lesson: it challenges the assumption that the problems faced by older migrant black people will be of a temporary nature, or that the next generation of British-born black people will face diminished problems of racism and disadvantage; it also demonstates that ethnic identities change but do not dissolve – indeed, they may be strengthened in times of adversity.

There is a need for some caution, however, in comparing the past experience of minority port communities with the present position of much larger migrant groups in a range of different industrial towns and cities: to begin with, history may not repeat itself and never does so exactly, and the motivations and economic background of many migrants of the 1950s and 1960s were quite different from the international, merchant shipping base of the port communities.

Nevertheless, the early history of such communities in Cardiff and Liverpool does show the precariousness of the black or Asian migrant's position in society and the danger of permanent non-acceptance. Also, having roots in another country or culture strengthens identity and may help to protect migrants from the psychological damage of racism. But, on the other hand, it may emphasize the temporary or 'guestworker' status of a minority.

A survey of the situation of older migrants in 13 European countries (EURAG 1987) strikingly illustrates how the citizenship and residence rights of many minorities are severely restricted. In the reports on almost every country, there are calls for the adoption of policies to permit foreign workers to move freely between their host and home countries, or to be able to transfer pension rights to their old countries. In Germany a Turkish worker, for example, may stay for an unlimited period in the country after five years of work. But if migrants return to Turkey for more than six months, retirement benefits are lost; also, foreign workers do not have the same social security rights as German citizens, and German citizenship is conditional rather than guaranteed (EURAG 1987: 46).

Not only do national policies vary upon questions of immigration, citizenship and minority rights, but the identity of a minority is also affected by particular historical events and emerging social relationships between minority and majority. Van Amersfoort (1982) brings this out well by comparing minority group formation in the Netherlands. The identities of each of the main Dutch minorities (the Indonesian Dutch, Ambonese/South Moluccans, Surinamese, and other foreign groups such as the Turks) have evolved out of a complex interaction between political events (for example, Indonesia's rejection of Moluccan independence) and social change in each community or among the majority. Similarly, Peach (1991) shows how Caribbean migrant communities in Britain, France and the Netherlands have attained markedly different social identities and occupy different economic or occupational niches in each country.

In order to help make sense of a potentially bewildering array of majority–minority relationships, it is worth considering the helpful distinctions made by Ogbu (1978) between 'caste-like', 'immigrant' and 'autonomous' minorities. These not only offer a model of minority relations in general but also help explain the particular position of Asian and Afro-Caribbean communities in Britain (see Chapters 5 and 6).

Ogbu's examples of 'caste-like' minorities include black or African Americans, native Americans and Latino minorities. 'Immigrant minorities' in the USA are exemplified by Eastern Asians such as the Chinese, Japanese and Korean Americans, while according to Ogbu 'autonomous' minorities would include the Jewish and Irish communities, people with Southern European ancestries, and some religious minorities which have distinctive ways of life, such as the Amish and Mormons. 'Autonomous' minorities have achieved a status of respected difference from the majority. They are no longer openly discriminated against and are formally regarded as equal to those in the majority, whereas members of immigrant and caste-like minorities are subject to open discrimination and may have difficulty in establishing their formal rights.

Over time, a minority's status may change (as arguably the Irish Americans' has) from, for example, 'immigrant' to 'autonomous'. Such changes will depend as much on the attitudes and policies of the majority as upon the actions of the minority. Ogbu also intends the identification of a particular minority with a 'type' to be as much a matter of debate as of straightforward classification.

With some exceptions, Britain's Southern Asian communities come closest to Ogbu's 'immigrant' type. According to this model, the objective economic and status position of the minority may be low to intermediate, as shown by higher than average unemployment, or numbers in low-paid jobs. However, it is characteristic of the 'immigrant' minority (including the non-migrant second and third generations) to continue to define their aspirations and standard of living more in relation to their ancestral or old country than to the majority in the host country.

Typically, the 'immigrant' community consists mainly of labour migrants in the first instance and, although the community may become a settled one as families with children take root, a primary goal of maintaining links with the old country remains: remitting money, keeping in touch with relatives and exchanging marriage partners, for example.

If 'immigrant' minority identity is maintained, at least for the foreseeable future, the implications for older people are that many of the protective aspects of community membership will also be kept, though there are also negative and restrictive aspects of community life, especially for women (see Chapter 6). However, a fundamental change – for example, to 'autonomous' minority status such as that attained by the Jewish community – could spell the break-up of existing community supports. They could well be replaced by other more institutionalized forms of care (as the example of the growth of Jewish old people's homes illustrates), and for the older members of the community there would be a potentially stressful period as family obligations and roles are renegotiated.

Whether or not the Asian communities will have, or want, a 'Jewish' future is, however, still an open question. If unemployment rates remain high and other racial disadvantages continue to blight the lives of younger Asians, then at least some minorities could shift, over time, from 'immigrant' to 'caste-like' status. By this term, Ogbu was referring to the permanently depressed position of certain minority groups (in the USA, African Americans, Latinos and native Americans). He maintains that a hidden 'job ceiling' effectively bars most people in caste-like minorities from higher-paid jobs, or any employment requiring higher educational qualifications. Despite some educational success, a sense of frustration and alienation is bound to grow among younger generations, occasionally resulting in social conflict and often in individual repudiation of the law and of majority values.

The effect of growing old in a 'caste-like' minority, if this term is applicable to the Afro-Caribbean community and certain Asian communities in Britain, is unclear. Inter-generational conflict is likely to increase if the second and third generations find themselves being pushed towards a 'caste-like' status while the older migrant generation cling to an 'immigrant' minority identity. For example, older Caribbean people will often see the West Indies as 'home', even if they never return permanently, while the younger British-born generations find less meaning in this (though for some, Rastafarian beliefs offer a pan-African identity). And though the older migrant generation included some actively radical men and women, they are more likely to be seen by their younger descendants as taking a resigned attitude towards racial injustice, and favouring a 'keeping your head down' approach to life.

Whether these attitudes will prevail in Britain remains to be seen, however. The possibility of an 'abandoned' older migrant generation questions notions of 'cohort self-sufficiency', or self-help within communities, discussed by Rowland (1991: 56). Such a prospect would certainly contrast with the image of an 'immigrant' minority which continues to provide support for its older members. But even if inter-generational differences do grow among Afro-Caribbean and Asian communities, it is not certain that they will be sufficient to undermine reciprocal care (grandparents child-minding their grand-children, or middle-aged daughters looking after ageing relatives). Some evidence from the United States shows that caring and other social relation-ships between older and younger black people stand the test of time *better* than among whites (see Chapter 4), suggesting that 'caste-like' minority status need not have a negative effect.

However, we should remember that the international migration of black migrants to Britain, and the subsequent development of their community, is quite different from the background of African Americans. Of greater significance, perhaps, are associations between 'caste-like' status, blocked opportunities and low income. Poverty and adverse living conditions among many black people in both countries have a more direct impact on health and quality of life in old age (see Chapter 4).

Conclusion

Comparative evidence shows that older black and Asian people in Britain face an open future. Though each community is bound to change, with nuclear family living and the adoption of some 'Western' values becoming more common, it may not be helpful to describe such change as a common 'modernization' process with attendant losses of status by older people. Some minority ethnic communities demonstrate a surprising degree of resilience, adapting traditions and family structures but retaining core values and making care of older people a priority; in others, there is inter-generational conflict and a loss of community identity.

Becoming aware that there are many different kinds of relationship between ethnic majorities and minorities reinforces the idea that older people in minorities face many possible futures. For example, there are parallels if not exact similarities between 'autonomous', 'immigrant' and 'caste-like' minori-ties in Britain and elsewhere. So while there are common problems of racial discrimination and social disadvantage, older black and Asian people in Britain will not share a common future. Differences among the communities, and in their emerging relationships with the majority, will ensure that.

4

Double jeopardy?

Discussion of ageing, race and ethnicity in Britain has been almost entirely focused on the problem of inequality and the additional disadvantages faced by older Asian and Afro-Caribbean people. Along with this has gone a desire to concentrate discussion on policy outcomes or the apparent failure of care providers to meet the needs of older black people.

These concerns are highly important, and the time has come to review the real meanings of the concepts of inequality in use. It is not enough to announce that inequality exists; it is also necessary to clarify its nature. Only then will policy changes be considered imaginatively and sensitively.

The term 'double jeopardy' has often been used to summarize the position of older black people, chiefly as a result of research carried out in the USA. The hypothesis was first stated by the National Urban League (1964), suggesting the twofold handicap of age and race discrimination and focusing on the disadvantages of income and ill health experienced by older blacks. Different indicators of inequalities between ageing black and white people have been used in subsequent American research, but they may be grouped as income inequalities; inequalities in life expectancy and disease; inequalities in social support by family, neighbours and friends; inequalities in life satisfaction, self-esteem, morale and psychological well-being.

Dowd and Bengston (1978: 427) suggest that older people in minorities are vulnerable because they

bear, in effect, a double burden. Like other older people in industrial societies, they experience the devaluation of old age found in most modern societies . . . Unlike other older people, however, the minority aged must bear the additional economic, social and psychological burdens of living in a society in which racial equality remains . . . a myth.

In Britain, the term has been applied rather loosely. Mays (1983: 73), for

Do older black people experience double jeopardy in social support and life satisfaction?
Photograph: Abdullah Badwi

example, provides a brief definition of double jeopardy which is accurate enough as far as it goes but which does not convey the full meaning of the concept as it has been applied in the American research. Norman (1985), in an otherwise useful empirical survey of local initiatives in social provision, uses the term 'triple jeopardy' in a somewhat idiosyncratic way which does not build upon earlier conceptual advances. Triple jeopardy refers to people being 'at risk because they are old, because of the physical conditions and hostility under which they have to live, and because services are not accessible to them' (1985: 1).

Yet triple jeopardy has more usually been defined as the combined impact of race, age and social class on the lives of people in disadvantaged minorities (see, for example, Jackson *et al.* 1982: 78). Norman's preliminary definition, on the other hand, conflates causes of disadvantage (age, race and hostility) with the outcomes of that inequality ('physical conditions', 'services . . . not accessible'). Thus age, race and social class are neither conceptually nor empirically separated. This is a pity, because Norman's comprehensive survey of service provision includes examples of white minority ethnic groups (such as Irish and Cypriot immigrants) and the analysis could have examined much more systematically than it did the distinct contributions of race, age and class discrimination.

The point of using such terms as double or triple jeopardy – or multiple hazard, which indicates an even more disadvantaged position resulting from other factors such as sex discrimination – is, as Jackson *et al.* (1982: 78) point out, not simply to state the 'facts' about the lives of older blacks or minorities but rather to provide 'a way of organizing the facts' as a 'step toward the development of a theory of black or minority ageing and of ageing in general'.

However, what little discussion there has been in Britain tends to assume that the term double jeopardy is simply a convenient label for the facts; rarely, if ever, has double jeopardy been discussed as a concept for building hypotheses or developing a more sensitive recognition of the heterogeneity of the minority ethnic population.

Demonstrating double jeopardy is a matter of describing not only racial inequalities between black and white old people at a particular time, but also how the overall position of each group has changed since a younger age. The hypothesis of double jeopardy therefore contains a dynamic element which has seldom been referred to in the British literature. As Bengston (1979: 20) points out:

> The relative numbers of ethnic minority aged having good health and adequate income may be less than those of aged whites. If, however, the percentage differences between middle-aged blacks and Mexican-Americans and their white counterparts are greater yet, a characterization of the minority aged as being in double jeopardy would be an incomplete description. It may be that age exerts a *levelling* influence on the ethnic differences found among younger cohorts.

Measuring inequalities over time by means of a longitudinal survey of ageing black and white people therefore offers us the best way of isolating the effects of age from race or ethnicity. Unfortunately, Dowd and Bengston's own study

(1978) did not employ longitudinal analysis but examined differences between three age groups (45–54, 55–64 and 65–74 years) of Mexican American, white and black people at a given time – a 'snapshot' picture of three age groups.

Therefore, though the study provides some important insights, the differences between the age groups could be partially influenced by age-related factors such as membership of a particular cohort, or by historical period effects, as well as by the process of ageing itself. For example, poorer health among an older group might be less a reflection of age and more to do with having experienced harsher migratory or occupational histories than the younger. In Britain differences between 'pioneer' migrants, who arrived before or around the time of the Second World War, and later migrants are much greater than the differences caused by the ageing process itself (Barker 1984: 19–20). As the more recent migrants age, their experiences of becoming and being old will be different from the earlier ones' experiences, affected as they were by a different history and different sets of circumstances.

Also, period effects complicate the picture. Though two ethnic groups may inhabit the same country and age through the same period of time, it does not follow that each has been influenced by the same processes of social change: 'what may be a period of dramatic change for one part of society may be stability or stagnation for another!' (Schaie *et al.* 1982: 224).

In summary, demonstrating the existence of double jeopardy is a rather complex task. To be convincing, it requires a methodology which allows the researcher to control for socio-economic status, sex and other characteristics if the specific impacts of race and age difference are to be isolated. Ideally it requires a longitudinal approach so that, as the same individuals are followed through time, cohort and period effects can be controlled.

American research on double jeopardy

Burton and Bengston (1982), commenting on American studies of ethnicity, ageing and double jeopardy, provide some explanations for the contradictory findings that have emerged. They conclude there may have been a tendency to overestimate and romanticize the role of the extended family and of support networks among minority communities, thus creating false impressions that in these respects the minority old are not all that disadvantaged. Another bias arises from 'the preoccupation with deviance from the white norm' (1982: 217) – that is, an overconcentration on cultural differences from the majority rather than focusing on issues of greater concern to the researched themselves, such as improving access to health care.

However, perhaps we should not take too sceptical a view of the American research. Because there is a much more comprehensive collection of information on the relative position of ethnic and racial groups in the USA, American studies illustrate the potential for future basic research in Britain. A second reason for paying heed to American evidence is that, though any two or three findings may seem inconclusive or contradictory, reasonably reliable conclusions can be drawn from the large number of studies conducted independently of each other.

In an overview of the literature, Jackson *et al.* (1982: 79) conclude that studies of double jeopardy in America commonly find that 'older blacks are doubly disadvantaged in income and physical health, but not in terms of mental health'. Another common finding is that inequalities in material conditions (for example, income, housing, urban environment) tend to widen between black and white people as they age. But blacks may not be especially disadvantaged in other respects, such as integration in family and friendship networks or psychological well-being, or life satisfaction.

Confirming this pattern, Dowd and Bengston (1978: 430) found that older black or African Americans are likely to suffer double jeopardy with regard to income and 'were significantly more likely to report poorer health than white respondents even with the effects of socio-economic status, sex and income held constant'.

However, with regard to familial interaction, they conclude that age exerts a levelling influence as white people have the lowest frequency of contact with relatives in old age, compared with black people and Mexican Americans (1978: 432). Life-satisfaction measures of tranquillity and optimism revealed no disadvantages as far as blacks were concerned, though older Mexican Americans had lower optimism scores than whites, whose scores decreased only slightly at increased ages.

Kent's (1971) 'age-as-leveller' theory suggests that age exerts a levelling influence on the ethnic differences found among younger cohorts. Thus, irrespective of ethnic identity, people in old age are subject to a variety of influences which cut across racial lines and may level differences in ageing patterns.

Does the American research suggest that the evidence for age levelling is stronger than for double jeopardy? In some respects it does, though the above research by Dowd, Bengston and others indicates a mixed picture, with material and health inequalities showing the clearest evidence of double jeopardy. It comes as something of a surprise, then, to find that in the USA death rates among white and black people, which are significantly unequal in middle age, tend to become more equal in old age – a levelling effect.

The 'racial crossover' in mortality rates

According to Manton (1982: 63), probabilities of death among whites and blacks reach a peak differential in middle age. It is well known in Britain that exposure to environmental and occupational hazards, poor housing and inadequate health care contribute towards higher chances of early death among lower social class groups (Townsend and Davidson 1982). Combined with racial discrimination and inequality, similar factors in the USA have caused a much higher death rate among American black people than among whites. But after middle age these racial inequalities decline sharply until 'non-white probabilities of death actually fall below the probabilities of death for whites over the age of 75' (Manton 1982: 63). This is the so-called 'racial crossover' in life expectancy, a subject which has led to heated discussion in the USA.

Jackson (1980: 84) takes issue with the idea that the racial crossover might be explained by innate or biological differences in ageing between races; environmental differences seem to carry more weight. Also, there have been suggestions that errors in age reporting and census enumeration have underestimated mortality rates among older blacks. Yet according to both Manton (1982) and Jackson (1980), mortality differentials are still observed to decline even when errors are taken into account. Not only have death rates in each category (black, white and other) been declining since the turn of the century, but also racial gaps in longevity have been narrowing (Jackson 1980).

Why does the American evidence on *mortality* rates indicate a decline in racial inequalities, when other aspects of inequality, notably *health*, seem to show the persistence of double jeopardy? One possibility is that historical improvements in social security, education and health services in the mid-twentieth century may have helped to narrow racial differences in death rates in old age, if not at younger ages so much. A more likely explanation is that mortality rates are not accurate indicators of general health. It is possible for a group to live longer, on average, than it did before. But the extra years lived might include a considerable amount of illness, and this is what the American evidence on black people's experience seems to show.

Finally, in considering the American evidence on double jeopardy as a whole, the social context in which older Americans live must be borne in mind. Not only does the economic and social policy context differ, but also attitudes to race relations, ethnicity and old age differ markedly between the USA, Britain and other European countries. Within the USA itself there are wide differences in historical patterns of migration and employment. For example, while many of the minority old in the USA have been born in that country whereas most of Europe's minority old people are relatively recent immigrants, there are important exceptions to this generalization on both sides of the Atlantic. The United States forms a vast and ethnically diverse country, and more pertinent observations are perhaps best made by restricting comparisons to selected states or geographical areas, or particular examples of minority–majority relations.

The British evidence

Studies of the position of older Asian and Afro-Caribbean people in British society have not set out to test for double jeopardy in the way American researchers have, but there is partial and indirect British evidence to support *some* of the conclusions reached in the United States. However, it is still too early to make definitive conclusions about the extent and nature of these inequalities.

For example, there is the question of whether, as with black Americans, there is a higher death rate among Afro-Caribbean and Asian people from middle age onwards, when compared with white people in equivalent socio-economic groups. But while America's black community is centuries old and there are entrenched patterns of racial inequality in health, the older migrants we are concerned with have in the main only been in Britain for between 15 and 30 years. As Townsend *et al.* (1988: 51) put it: 'Men and women prepared to cross oceans and continents in order to seek new opportunities . . . do not represent a cross-section of humanity'.

As they point out, migrants tend to have been of better health than the average in the populations they have left – a characteristic confirmed by Marmot *et al*.'s (1984) comparison of death rates among migrants to Britain with death rates in their countries of origin. This will offset significantly the adverse and health-threatening conditions black and Asian migrants often confront in Britain: the combined effect of all the factors which create double jeopardy, such as poverty, hazardous working conditions, and stress caused by unemployment or the threat of racism.

It is perhaps less surprising than it might first appear, then, to find that according to rather early (1972) OPCS data, mortality rates among black and Asian migrants in social classes IV and V were actually *lower* than among white people of the same social classes, though this advantage disappears when black people higher up the social scale are compared with their white equivalents (Townsend and Davidson 1982: 59).

In addition to the favourable effect of being a self-selected group with somewhat better health to begin with, it has been suggested that some minority communities have lifestyles which increase life expectancy. Assuming such factors are significant, they would again counteract the risks of double jeopardy. For example, Balarajan and Yuen (1984) found lower than expected mortality from diseases related to smoking (notably lung cancer, other cancers, bronchitis) among people from the Indian subcontinent. Though customs vary and there are significant differences in smoking and drinking habits between men and women, and between ethnoreligious groups (Sikhs, Hindus, Muslims), as a whole older Asians have been protected from the risks of death from smoking and excessive alcohol consumption.

The same survey and the evidence summarized by Whitehead (1988) shows that deaths from other causes common in Britain – especially various types of cancer – are significantly fewer among black and Asian migrants. Therefore, there is no clear evidence yet that double jeopardy exists, as far as mortality is concerned, for the black and Asian community as a whole.

However, this is not the end of the story, for a number of reasons. First, there are worrying signs of higher than expected rates of mortality for certain diseases in certain communities. As Balarajan and others have noted, for example, there is a relatively high rate of death from coronary heart disease among Asians despite lower incidence of smoking and drinking alcohol (see also Chapter 7). Asians also experience higher than expected mortality from cardiovascular disease, diabetes, tuberculosis and other infective diseases, and liver cancer (Whitehead 1988). Migrants from the Caribbean are much more likely to die from strokes/cardiovascular disease, liver cancer, the complications resulting from diabetes, and from accidents than people in the majority population.

Therefore although double jeopardy may not be apparent when the sum totals of mortality are compared between the minorities and the majority, there is clear evidence of added risk of death or jeopardy as far as certain troublesome diseases are concerned. If preventive measures against coronary heart disease are less successful among the minority communities than among the white majority, for example, this particular and important health inequality will continue to widen.

Second, we should remember that the data upon which the above conclusions are based were collected in the 1970s, when the Asian and Afro-Caribbean migrant community was that much younger than it is now. Admittedly the comparisons of mortality rates between the minority ethnic groups and the majority were age-standardized, so that 50-year-olds were compared with 50-year-olds, and so on, but in the early 1970s the number of Afro-Caribbeans and Asians aged over 50 was very small – perhaps too small a group of mainly 'pioneer' migrants to be basing firm generalizations upon. And those *now* in their sixties and seventies will include a far higher proportion who have lived in Britain for most of their working lives, perhaps making them more susceptible to 'double jeopardy' influences and less likely to be protected by the factors which tend to keep migrants' health at a higher than average level – though this possibility needs further investigation.

And third, as we pointed out in relation to the American evidence, it is quite possible for a minority's *mortality* rates to be lower than in the majority population, but for its rates of *illness* to be higher than average. Most experiences of illness, even in old age, are not immediately life-threatening.

We further discuss patterns of health and illness among older Asians and Afro-Caribbeans in Chapter 7. Before that, however, it is appropriate to consider briefly the double jeopardy thesis in relation to other aspects of inequality in health – as expressed both in terms of patterns of use of health services and self-identified health problems; to this evidence we will also add a discussion of inequality under the headings of income, and of life satisfaction and social support, following the themes in the American research. However, only selected major research findings will be discussed in this chapter and in the main we will restrict ourselves to comparison between minority older people and the white majority. More detailed discussion of health, living circumstances, social support and other issues will follow in later chapters.

Other health inequalities

The issue of the health of minority ethnic groups, as compared with that of the general population, is a sensitive one. Competing claims that minorities are either healthier or that they experience more illness than the average are difficult to verify. It is certainly not true that Asian or Afro-Caribbean people make excessive use of the health service or place unreasonable demands on it (Mark Johnson 1986: 205) and, summarizing what evidence we do have on ethnic minorities' use of health services, the Runnymede Trust (1980: 109) concluded that use is 'primarily a consequence of their socio-economic circumstances and certainly not because they are physically different from the majority'.

There is a danger of 'blaming the victim' when discussing the health of black people or their use of medical services; this form of racism places undue stress on either biological and genetic or on 'pathological' cultural factors as explanations for health problems, but neglects the shortcomings of health services providers (Mares *et al.* 1985).

Table 4.1 GP consultations among Asian, Afro-Caribbean and white older people (percentages)

Last visit to GP	Asians			Afro-Caribbeans			Whites		
	Women	Men	Total	Women	Men	Total	Women	Men	Total
Within last month	66	72	70 (67)	75	59	69	48	65	53 (30)
1–12 months	24	21	22 (28)	21	28	23	26	18	23 (50)
Longer/never	10	7	8 (5)	4	13	8	26	17	24 (20)
N	62	107	169	111	68	179	35	17	52

Note: Percentages in brackets derived from Donaldson (1986: 1081)
Source: AFFOR (1981); Donaldson (1986)

One study of health among older Asians and Afro-Caribbeans, most of whom, it will be recalled, are 'young old', suggested they are already experiencing levels of illness comparable with significantly older whites (Blakemore 1982). According to these findings, illness inequalities seem set to increase with age, though this is not an absolute certainty for every ethnic group.

More generally, there are two main types of evidence on health and illness to be drawn from British studies: first, evidence on rates of use of health services (GPs, hospital and health visiting or district nursing services); and second, evidence from self-reported observations of illness.

Health services – access and use

A number of researchers have agreed that older Asian and Afro-Caribbean people need to visit their GPs for medical treatment significantly more often than do the majority of older people (for example, Ebrahim *et al.* 1991). As this and other studies report little inappropriate use of medical services by people in the minority communities, it can be assumed that higher consultation rates do indicate objectively higher incidence rates of health problems.

In Birmingham, we found that over two-thirds of the Asians and Afro-Caribbeans had visited their GP during the month before the interview, compared to about half of the older white group in the same inner-city neighbourhoods (see Table 4.1). These findings are close to those of Donaldson (1986) in a study of GP consultations by Asian and white older people.

It is worth noting that rates of consultation among the *white* elderly sample interviewed by AFFOR are relatively high in comparison with the population as a whole, reflecting a rather depressed level of health in the inner cities. For example, the Central Statistical Office (1980) reported about the time of the AFFOR survey that two-thirds of all British women and slightly fewer men (63 per cent) in the 65–74 age group had seen a doctor in the previous year. This compares with 74 per cent of women and 83 per cent of men, respectively, in the AFFOR sample.

The implication of poorer health among older white people in inner cities is that if older black people's health and use of medical services are compared to the national picture, rather than to local whites, the position of the minorities looks even more disadvantaged.

One possible cause of relatively high rates of GP consultation, at least among Asian patients, is a lower than expected rate of hospital admission (see Table 4.2). GPs in some areas are coping with a considerable amount of illness which older Asians might otherwise seek hospital treatment for, suggesting that both delays in referral to hospital and fears of hospitalization among Asians increase risks of inadequate treatment.

According to the Birmingham (Bhalla and Blakemore 1981) evidence, almost a third of older Asians reported multiple health problems (three or four complaints concerning sight, hearing, mobility, dental health and other problems such as heart disease). On the other hand Ebrahim *et al.* (1987) concluded that while the older Asian patients they surveyed were more at risk from some diseases than older whites (see Chapter 7), their overall health was

Table 4.2 Visits to hospital during the previous 12 months, among Afro-Caribbean, Asian and white older people (percentages)

Visits in 12 months up to date of interview	Asians			Afro-Caribbeans			Whites		
	Women	Men	Total	Women	Men	Total	Women	Men	Total
Once	18	18	18	23	24	23	23	6	17
Twice	5	4	4	9	7	8	0	12	4
Three times or more	3	3	3	12	5	12	6	11	8
Never/don't know	74	75	75	56	64	57	71	71	71
Spent 1+ nights in hospital	11	14	13	21	19	20	11	24	15
Total	100	100	100	100	100	100	100	100	100
N	62	107	169	111	68	179	35	17	52

Source: AFFOR (1981)

not significantly worse. Their Leicester survey did *not* find that Asian older people are less likely than whites to be admitted to hospital, even controlling for need or urgency of treatment; nor was it found that ineffective treatment occurred more often among Asian patients.

Geographical, social class and ethnic factors are almost certainly at work in this case, reducing or removing risks of double jeopardy in health. The high proportion of Asian people of East African origin in Leicester, many of whom have relatively high expectations of their health and of health services, will have influenced the picture. Similar conclusions are reached in a later study by Ebrahim *et al.* (1991) of older Gujaratis in north London: as they point out, many of these old Asians are economically better off than local white people, though they do identify some worrying disease trends among the Asians such as higher rates of myocardial infarction among older men, diabetes among older women, and stroke and asthma among men and women, compared with indigenous patients.

Fenton (1986) found evidence of both poorer health and significantly less use of hospitals by Asians in a relatively 'young' Bristol community of Asian middle-aged/older people from a variety of ethnic backgrounds, confirming that ethnic and regional variations are highly significant. He concluded that older white people are more advantaged than Asians in obtaining referrals for hospital treatment (1986: 52).

The Afro-Caribbeans stand out as the group who have been hospitalized most often. We found, in Birmingham (AFFOR 1981), that the difference between them and the white Asian rates of hospitalization is statistically significant ($p < 0.001$). But as with GP services, it is the high proportion of Afro-Caribbean *women* who had visited hospital and/or been hospitalized which accounts for this difference. Though Afro-Caribbean men in Birmingham were more at risk of needing hospital treatment than the Asian and white groups, the difference was not significant.

Self-reported illness

The major community surveys confirm a picture of a relatively high incidence of illness if we take into account responses to survey questions which asked respondents about their own health, though there are significant differences between the sexes and age groups, and between minority communities. For example, the Bristol survey (Fenton 1987) found very high proportions reporting serious problems of one kind or another – two-thirds of the Afro-Caribbeans aged over 60 and half of those aged 45–59.

Asking respondents about medical problems in a different way, the Birmingham study (AFFOR 1981) identified four problems with physical functioning (sight, hearing, walking/mobility, dental). It was discovered that only 18 per cent of Afro-Caribbeans and 23 per cent of whites (a much older group) were free of such problems, though 30 per cent of Asians reported being so (Blakemore 1982). It must be remembered, however, that the Birmingham Asian community included both 'extremes': the highest proportion mentioning multiple health problems (32 per cent) as well as the highest proportion without any of the four functioning problems.

To summarize, the evidence we have on health and illness among older people of minority ethnic groups, compared to older white people, suggests complex patterns and differences between ethnic groups and males and females of the various groups. To say that there is double jeopardy in health in every minority community and age group would be too sweeping. However, there are no clear signs that age is acting as a leveller of differences in illness rates between ethnic or racial groups; rather, there are ominous signs that in poorer and industrial communities (as distinct from better-off communities in Leicester and London) older black and Asian people in Britain will experience rising racial inequalities in health.

Income inequalities

There is common agreement in all the community surveys of older Asian and Afro-Caribbean people that poverty is a sharp problem for many of them. But are older black people sharing a similar level of income with local white, mainly working-class older people, or are they more economically deprived than that?

The Birmingham survey provides information on income which is now rather dated, but does show that while two-fifths of black older people lived on the lowest income level, less than a fifth of white elderly people did so (see Table 4.3).

Other studies, though not always making direct comparisons between white and black older people, also suggest that for a variety of reasons old Asians and Afro-Caribbeans are more likely than their white counterparts to experience a lowering of income to below the average for all the retired (Barker 1984; Fenton 1987). In particular, the position of older Asian women, who may neither receive all the pension or welfare benefits to which they are entitled, nor share at all in the property rights of husbands or male relatives, can easily be overlooked. Boneham (1987: 325) concludes in her study of older Sikh women that 'the results are definitive that ethnic minority older people are worse off than the indigenous population in terms of income and use of social services'.

Kippax (1978) found more than 25 per cent of minority older people were receiving less than their full benefits and 25 per cent were not aware of bus passes. Pride or embarrassment may be a reason shared with indigenous older people, but added to this, for the Asians, is an ignorance of the system because of language problems and low expectations regarding their general rights to financial benefits (Glendenning 1979: 58–9).

As discussed in Chapter 2, not all black workers arriving between the 1940s and 1960s fell into a common underclass, and the Birmingham data on income in old age suggest that a small minority (more among Asians than Afro-Caribbeans – see Table 4.3) are better off than the average old person in an inner-city area. Yet their chances of promotion at work, of obtaining employment with average rates of pay, or skilled jobs would in many cases have been seriously affected by racial discrimination by employers (Smith 1977; Braham *et al.* 1981).

More recently, as rates of unemployment spiralled upwards in the recession

Table 4.3   Weekly income of older Afro-Caribbeans, Asians and whites in Birmingham (percentages)

Weekly income	Afro-Caribbeans	Asians	Whites
Under £20	42	38	17
£20–£40	49	47	79
£41+	9	15	4
N	179	169	52

Source: Bhalla and Blakemore (1981: 19)

of the West Midlands, North of England and even parts of London, the pressure of redundancy has combined with, even outweighed, the effects of racial discrimination in employment (Cross 1987). Fenton (1987) remarks on a growing number of black people in their forties and fifties who have been made redundant and, unlikely to be re-employed permanently, are in a roleless position of 'waiting to be elderly'.

In summarizing the evidence on income inequalities, therefore, we must bear in mind not only objective indices of disadvantage but also feelings of a loss of a potential future or of financial security in old age. These subjective factors will in some cases increase the disadvantages of double jeopardy by adding psychological stress to material deprivation.

Inequalities in life satisfaction and social support

Previous research on subjective and 'quality of life' aspects of growing old led to serious questioning of the methodology used to find out about how people feel about their lives and their relationships with family, friends and others (Larson 1978; Burton and Bengston 1982; Palmore 1983). Cross-cultural comparisons easily lead to misunderstanding, but particularly so when the object of study is something as difficult to define as life satisfaction. And though social support might at first appear to be more amenable to objective evaluation than life satisfaction, there are uncertainties about how to assess the quality of support and how to judge whether one group is better supported than another.

Despite these difficulties, we argue that it would be a mistake to leave out any consideration of such important aspects of ageing, as they are of central concern to the question of whether older black people face double jeopardy or whether inequalities diminish with age. However, given the heterogeneity of the older population in minority ethnic groups, conclusions should be regarded as tentative.

A strong sense of loss emerges from the community surveys of older Afro-Caribbeans and Asians in Britain. But there have not yet been any systematic attempts to measure life satisfaction among Britain's minority older people, at least in the ways employed by Dowd and Bengston (1978) or Abrams (1978). Yet the early surveys by Berry *et al.* (1981), Bhalla and Blakemore (1981) and Barker (1984) all threw up important findings – for example, on the desire to return 'home', on fears of racial victimization, or on worries about rapid change in family life and its effects on inter-generational relations – which suggest that an evaluation of life satisfaction and social support in old age is necessary.

In assessing the likelihood of double jeopardy, it is important to keep an open mind. The American research, as outlined above, indicates that it is *not* a foregone conclusion that older people in minority ethnic groups are worse off than the majority as far as either life satisfaction or social support are concerned.

Depending on the ethnic groups in question, the position of the minority elderly may even improve with age, relative to that of majority white older people. As mentioned in the previous chapter, other work (Cool 1980; 1981; Hazan 1980; Holzberg 1982) has indicated that in some respects a distinct ethnic identity is a valuable resource in old age, offering elements of continuity through the life course and ways of maintaining personal identity and self-esteem.

Life satisfaction and attitudes to living in Britain

Looking first at the attitudes of older Afro-Caribbeans in Britain, the Birmingham survey (AFFOR 1981) showed that they are more likely to express dissatisfaction with their circumstances than either older Asian or white older people. In response to various questions, only a third of the Afro-Caribbeans responded with satisfaction, while two-thirds of Asians and whites expressed satisfaction (Blakemore 1985a: 96).

This finding should *not* be interpreted as a statement that 'most West Indian people are dissatisfied with all aspects of their lives' or that 'all old Asian people are content with their lives in Britain'. Yet the finding, though it masks all kinds of differences within and between ethnic groups, suggests that there may be a considerable gap between Afro-Caribbeans' and Asians' adjustment to old age in British society. As discussed in Chapter 2, few Afro-Caribbeans or Asians at any one time have definite plans to resettle in their countries of origin. However, the Birmingham survey disclosed that almost two-fifths of the Afro-Caribbeans expressed a wish to live in another country; only 16 per cent of the Asians expressed this preference. As Fenton (1987: 19) remarks on Afro-Caribbean older people in Bristol:

> We can now find older West Indians . . . who did not expect to spend their old age in Britain. The older they are the more likely they have become reconciled – at least in a minimal way – to the loss of the dream of return. Nonetheless even in this group the longing to be 'home' is very strongly expressed by many. In the rather younger elderly . . . the wish to return is often . . . still expressed as a real aspiration.

The social networks surrounding older Asians tend, with some exceptions, to be both denser and more extensive than those in which old Afro-Caribbeans live. Therefore it is possible, as we concluded in the Birmingham study, that Asians are more likely to have experienced some reinforcement of cultural identity in Britain and that this will provide a partial reassurance to 'stay, be cared for and die in Britain' (Bhalla and Blakemore 1981: 46).

A sense of loss?

This is not to say that many among the Asian old do not experience considerable feelings of loss and separation from the societies in which they grew up (Anwar 1979). Cultural differences in answers to questions about satisfaction could also have influenced responses as well as real differences. As Boneham (1987) points out, Asian women are particularly disadvantaged by expectations of docility and passivity so that, if questioned in the presence of men or other women of the husband's family, they can be discouraged from voicing their true feelings. Boneham is convinced, from close observational study, that levels of dissatisfaction, including depression and loneliness, are seriously underestimated in previous surveys of the position of older Asian women.

However, broad differences between the social networks of Asians and Afro-Caribbeans do go some way towards accounting for differences in levels of life satisfaction. The nature of these social networks and of Asian families will be explored more fully in Chapter 6.

Double jeopardy in life satisfaction and social support?

Though we began by mentioning problems and difficulties of ageing, there is another side to the coin. As we said above, problems are by no means evenly experienced or reported among the ethnically heterogeneous Asian and Afro-Caribbean communities. More than a few minority older people are ageing 'successfully', whether we care to use subjective or outsiders' definitions of success.

Given such a complex picture, can any valid comparisons be made between the black experience of old age and levels of life satisfaction or social support among older whites? Taking the evidence on life satisfaction first, all would appear to depend on which group of older whites are to be used as the basis for comparison. It is when we draw comparisons between older Asians and Afro-Caribbeans, on the one hand, and older whites in *inner-city* environments, on the other, that it seems unreasonable to conclude that double jeopardy exists. Most of the older whites included in the Birmingham survey, for example, seem neither to be better-off in terms of life satisfaction now, nor likely to experience improvements in the future. They are representatives of a mainly downwardly mobile group of white people and, remaining in declining inner-city areas, have experienced significant losses of satisfaction and social status. They are disadvantaged in terms of social class (Phillipson 1982). Though some have a residual loyalty to their neighbourhoods, the older whites' views reflect a mixture of racialist resentment, powerlessness (having had no voice in directing the way 'their' neighbourhoods have changed) and of being trapped in an environment which seems to them to be less and less 'friendly' than it was (Blakemore 1983c).

Though some older whites are better-off than black people in material terms

– for example, a larger proportion inhabit dwellings with three or more rooms per person than either the Asian or Afro-Caribbean elderly (Bhalla and Blakemore 1981) – such 'advantages' can easily turn to worries about inability to maintain or repair property or, as difficulties in mobility increase, about the unsuitability of the house.

While inner-city white older people are not advantaged in terms of life satisfaction, neither do they enjoy any distinct advantage over older black people in social interaction or support. In Birmingham, for example, significantly fewer older whites than either Asians or Afro-Caribbeans have regular daily or weekly contact with friends or relatives (Table 4.4). These are interesting findings, in that American evidence showed that though older whites had the lowest frequency of contact with relatives, they had the *higher* levels of contact with friends and neighbours, compared with black and Mexican older people (Dowd and Bengston 1978: 433).

However, distinctions between 'relatives' and 'friends' are culturally relative and such differences might have affected the Birmingham survey, possibly boosting the contact Asians had with 'friends' already counted as relatives. Also, neither frequency of contact nor sheer numbers of people one is friendly with, or resides with, can be translated into quality of contact. Though older whites in Birmingham had the lowest frequencies of contact and more often lived alone than either Asians or Afro-Caribbeans (AFFOR 1981), this does not mean that as a result they experienced the severest losses of self-esteem or the most loneliness; such effects are filtered through cultural expectations and, as will be recalled from Cantor's (1976) study, the ethnic group with the most frequent contact between the generations may nevertheless report dissatisfaction with social relationships most often. It must also be remembered that the white older people with whom these comparisons are made were of an average age significantly greater than the average of the Asian and Afro-Caribbean groups. Could the differences in social interaction be better explained by age differences between black and whites than by race or ethnicity?

In fact, though the amount of contact and support received by older whites in inner-city Birmingham might appear to be relatively low, it matches closely the frequency of contact with friends and relatives reported in Abram's (1978: 30) general conclusions. Therefore the somewhat higher amount of contact among black and Asian older people stands out from the general population, not just from the local population, as a set of ethnic differences and a possible advantage in later life.

Conclusions

The evidence we have of inequalities between older black and white people is mixed. Though some old Asians and Afro-Caribbeans are clearly disadvantaged in important respects, notably in health and income, it is not yet clear whether these disadvantages become relatively greater or relatively less with age, compared to the process of ageing among white older people.

The lack of certainty is partly a result of the way research has been designed to date, with few direct comparisons between old black and white people who share the same environment, and partly because cohort effects make it

Table 4.4 Frequency of contact with friends and relatives among whites, Asians and Afro-Caribbeans (percentages)

	Whites		Asians		Afro-Caribbeans	
	Friends	*Relatives*	*Friends*	*Relatives*	*Friends*	*Relatives*
Daily or at least weekly	73	57	92	86	85	65
Less than weekly	27	43	8	14	15	35
N	52	52	169	169	172	172

Source: AFFOR (1981)

uncertain how ageing will affect people of Asian and Caribbean descent in the future – at the moment we are dealing mainly with 'first-generation' settlers whose experiences are distinct and varied.

A brief review of evidence on subjective aspects of ageing – life satisfaction and social contact – showed that, in their own ways, Asian, Afro-Caribbean and inner-city white older people all appear to be at risk from certain hazards to their well-being. If anything, it is the 'old old' inner-city whites who seem to be the most deprived in terms of frequent social contact with friends, neighbours and relatives, but many difficulties of interpretation surround the results.

Though rarely living alone and often well supported by their close relatives, it is possible to find some loneliness among older Asians, especially among older women. And a significant number of old Afro-Caribbeans, though often well supported by relatives and friends and finding satisfying social relationships in social clubs and churches, are strongly affected by feelings of being trapped in a country they would ideally like to leave.

These conclusions are advanced with a recognition that further research in different kinds of urban neighbourhood – for example, areas which include a wider variety of 'white' minority ethnic groups – could well yield yet more interesting and complex results. However the biggest step to be made is that of realizing the nature of the inequalities under discussion and the need for more sensitive, thorough comparative research than has hitherto been conducted, either in the USA or in Britain.

5

The Afro-Caribbeans' experience

Introduction

In any discussion of ageing it is important to hear the voice of older people themselves. In this and the next chapter we will try to draw together and give voice to the views and personal experiences of older Afro-Caribbean and Asian people. The views and 'voices' are taken from research which has recorded personal impressions and life histories (Blakemore 1984; Boneham 1987). Additional observations from other community studies, including those carried out in the years of peak immigration, will also be included.

Those who migrated from the West Indies and who are now aged between 55 and 75 are a unique generation. They are the representatives of the main influx of people from the Caribbean who entered Britain in the 1950s and early 1960s. They bore the brunt of the major adjustments faced by the first substantial post-war group of black migrants: finding accommodation, a job, bringing their children from the Caribbean to join them.

The personal accounts of these older people are an expression of social history as well as a set of individual life stories. The older people from Jamaica, St Kitts or Barbados have vivid memories of their island communities as they were before 1960. Though some came from urbanized communities, the majority started out in rural areas, usually growing up on smallholdings where their parents worked the land or were engaged in commerce or a trade.

Also, their recollection of London, Birmingham and other British cities in the 1950s and 1960s offer a fascinating insight into the history – some would say, the decline – of race relations.

Caribbean diversity

We cannot say, however, that the experiences of older Afro-Caribbeans now will provide a model of how future cohorts of Afro-Caribbeans will age. There are likely to be some continuities, such as a common experience of racial disadvantage among older and younger generations, or a sharing of certain cultural attributes – for example, language and use of *patois*, diet, and, among some, a strong interest in religion. But there are also considerable differences if not discontinuities between the generations (Foner 1979). There are even differences between those older black people now in their late sixties and seventies, many of whom came to Britain in middle age, and those who came at younger ages.

Inter-generational change will also result from shifting family and residence patterns in the Afro-Caribbean community and geographical mobility among the younger generation. Sometimes families are divided between Britain, the West Indies and other countries such as the USA. As Foner (1979: 171) notes, the 'middle-aged migrants' tend to have fewer family ties in Britain and will have left most of their close kin and other contacts in the old country, whereas the youngest migrant cohort and certainly the British-born 'second generation' have most of their family and friendship ties in Britain.

The Afro-Caribbean case therefore illustrates particularly well a general truth about ageing – that one generation's or cohort's experience of history and of old age will be different from that of succeeding cohorts. In addition, the older Afro-Caribbeans show us that 'ethnicity' and 'culture' are not static entities. The meaning of being 'West Indian' or 'Caribbean' is dependent on the life course one has experienced and the historical period in which one is located. For many older people, their background is an insular one (Lowenthal 1972: 213) and, though their island communities had extensive contacts with the outside world, their identification with the terms 'West Indian' or 'Afro-Caribbean' is relatively recent. Back 'home', they would have thought of themselves as Barbadians, Jamaicans, Trinidadians, or whatever, and in some circumstances still do so. Also among this cohort, antipathies toward other islanders would have been quite strong – a reflection of lack of knowledge of other islands (especially the French-, Dutch- and Spanish-influenced countries) and a lack of a common 'Caribbean' identity.

Among younger migrants, however, there have been different experiences: independence from colonial rule, the experience of the West Indies Federation (though short-lived) and the development of Black Consciousness and 'black' identity. The development of a common racial identity is yet more prevalent among the second and third generations, and has taken on new forms among the British-born.

So while an 'ethnic group' such as 'Afro-Caribbean' may be defined as one which shares a common past or history, it is important to remember that the past has different meanings for different age groups. Even contemporaries may disagree about the past, or about more recent events in the Caribbean. For example, some respondents in a Birmingham survey (Blakemore 1984) were very loyal to their old countries and would not hear a bad word said about them. But others spoke disparagingly about political and social change:

> We have no paradise to go to now. Right now, it's difficult over the whole world . . . since we leave Jamaica . . . I don't know, a hell . . . It was like another nation takin' over, killin' and robbin' . . .
>
> Mr G

The diversity of experiences and opinions among older Afro-Caribbeans demonstrates that this is not a homogeneous minority ethnic group. And though there are some strong bonds of common culture and religion among Afro-Caribbeans, the life of the older people now should be viewed as something located in a relatively circumscribed historical period: in other words, as a rather distinct and precarious thing that will not be replicated.

This sense of historical uniqueness was brought home to the author (Blakemore 1984) on a particular visit to an older woman from Jamaica. Her living room in a small apartment was a haven from the busy traffic outside. The heavy ticking of a clock and the solid furniture emphasized the silence in the room. Her contacts with younger relatives were shown by fading photographs of nephews and nieces living in Canada and various parts of the Caribbean, and of a son and daughter in Britain. There was evidence, in the pictures and framed proverbs on the walls, of this respondent's religious faith, and of her love of sewing and embroidery in the work she was completing on the table, and in the fancy lace curtains.

All these and other things were small signs of a particular way of life for an elderly woman from the Caribbean in a late twentieth-century British city. It is quite possible, of course, to pick out the cultural preferences, tastes and attitudes of older people in any ethnic community – including older English people – and to note how the atmosphere they create in their homes will soon be gone. However, for the migrant generation, somewhat divided between their roots and memories of the old country and their ties to Britain, the transient position of older Afro-Caribbeans carries an added poignancy.

We hope to have established, in this introduction, that individual and personal experiences of ageing are important. They 'bring alive' the processes of social change and show how historical events have had particular impacts. At the same time, individual experience needs to be put in context. Without some understanding of social change and historical background, individual life histories have little resonance. In the next section, we will therefore highlight key aspects of (a) the social and historical background of the West Indies and (b) the migrant's experiences of life in Britain; we hope that this background will give a fuller understanding of individual cases and of the different categories of response by older Caribbeans to growing older in Britain.

Caribbean echoes

Caribbean society shaped the lives of black migrants before they came to Britain. The impact of that society – its economy, inequalities and culture – helps to explain why they came. Its influences continue to echo in the lives of the older migrants, affecting their views of the past and of present-day Caribbean society.

What were these key influences? First, and perhaps most important, was the impact of growing up in an 'emigrant society'. Rather like western Irish communities, Caribbean society has a long-established tradition of migration (Lowenthal 1972). In such societies it becomes the norm to leave the home community as a young man or woman – not necessarily to go overseas, but at least to find work in a larger town or city to support oneself. As a consequence, the home community usually becomes both outward-looking and stultifying or parochial at the same time. In villages, one's neighbours have relatives and other contacts in Kingston, London or New York, but nothing much happens in the village itself: small communities in small island economies lack amenities, whether cultural (entertainment, libraries, and so on), social (health facilities, education) or economic opportunities for work or investment (Lowenthal 1972: 215). These are factors which are bound to weigh in the mind when considering a permanent return 'home'.

Though there is much debate about the long-term impact of emigration on home communities, there is no doubt that the Caribbean 'migration boom' of the 1940s and 1950s caused considerable social upheavals. For example, Lowenthal (1972: 220) mentions the 'acute distress' caused in families during that time, when both older people and children were left without support by young adult migrants. Many of those migrants, now growing old themselves, have had to try to come to terms with the impact of their departure.

Migration from the West Indies in the post-war period was associated not only with demand for labour in the industrial world but also with a rapid decline in rural work opportunities. As Kuper (1976: 26) notes of Jamaica, for example, there has been a 'massive shift' of population from the rural areas to the rapidly growing towns, mining and tourist areas. Though farms in Jamaica tend to be small – about nine acres on average (Kuper 1976: 32) – and still provide the most important source of employment, agriculture as a whole has become less labour-intensive; rapid population growth since the 1920s has also meant that many have been forced to find work elsewhere.

As a result, according to Kuper (1976: 31), it is a 'striking feature of rural employment in Jamaica that . . . it is biased in favour of older people'. According to a government survey the *average* age of Jamaican farmers is over 50, and this in a population of which almost two-thirds are aged under 24. Here again the Irish parallel is striking: it is customary for farmers to retain control of their land well into old age – they are reluctant to transfer it to their heirs before death. The reasons for emigration, especially among young men, are therefore clear. But there is an implication that, after many years in another country such as Britain, land might suddenly become available again, though to what extent this will affect return migration will be unclear until larger numbers retire from work in Britain.

The first point to establish, therefore, is that older black people in Britain – both men and women – are likely to have come from rural backgrounds of restricted opportunity, where underemployment was high, work often seasonal and wages low. Despite social change and the growth of urban areas, nearly two-thirds of Jamaica's population, for example, is still rural.

It is true that migrants tend not to be representative of their own societies – they are usually more skilled, more often from towns and from non-agricultural working backgrounds. Quoting a mid-1950s Jamaican government survey of migrants (relevant to the period in which British Afro-Caribbeans were leaving), Patterson (1965: 69) showed that fewer than a quarter of men had been in farming or fishing (compared with over two-thirds of all employed) and that 31 per cent of men and 61 per cent of women had been working in 'manufacturing' (compared with 8 per cent of all).

To set against this we should be aware that 'manufacturing' most often refers to work in small-scale, informal sector concerns rather than in factories. Among women, for example, dressmakers and seamstresses were counted as employees in manufacturing. More importantly, the period of maximum migration from the West Indies to Britain, 1955–62, was, according to Peach (1991), unselective in terms of skills or qualifications. Direct recruitment of workers by British employers played a small if significant part, but the majority of migrants to Britain were not directly recruited, were semi-skilled and were often from agricultural backgrounds, as our case studies below demonstrate.

From a Caribbean perspective, Britain was a relatively unimportant migration destination except during the late 1940s and 1950s period. As Peach points out, there are 5 million in the various Caribbean communities in the United States, compared with half a million in Britain. The people going to the United States have tended to be more skilled and better educated than those who came to Britain before the mid-1960s.

Despite the lack of educational opportunities in the Caribbean islands in the 1940s and 1950s and consequent problems of illiteracy, contemporary commentators recorded the strong effect that schooling had on raising expectations. One effect was to promote an ideal view of Britain and the desirability of going there: the effect of 'generations of laudatory school books' in the days of Empire (Lowenthal 1972: 223).

The schooling of that generation also widened the 'formidable gap between reality and desire' (Smith 1973: 191). Aspirations, in the West Indies of those days, were very rarely for high-flying posts in government or the professions; they were for the 'ordinary' occupations that schoolchildren in Britain could realistically hope for, such as being a nurse, a teacher or a skilled mechanic. For all but a few West Indians of that generation, such occupations were unfulfilled dreams. Only one in twenty Jamaican children, for example, had a chance of secondary education at that time (Smith 1973: 195).

In addition to all this, one has to remember that the society from which Caribbean migrants came was, and remains, sharply divided by class and status distinctions. Various commentators have described this system of social inequality (for example, Lowenthal 1972; Foner 1973; Lowenthal and Comitas 1973) and it is not necessary for us to re-examine it in any detail. However it is important to note that status in Caribbean society is based on an interplay between race and class: there are subtle gradations of skin colour, with lighter-skinned people generally having higher status, and these operate together with observed material wealth, or poverty, and educational level.

Their significance lies in the fact that they are hard or impossible to 'shake off'. Though most migrants arrived in Britain wanting to go back to the old country, it was always with the expectation that they could return to demonstrate that they had achieved upward social mobility or had earned enough money to sustain a higher standard of living back 'home' (Lowenthal 1972: 230). Migration therefore offered not only the prospects of work at higher wages, but also a social escape from the local class system. Lowenthal (1972: 229) mentions, for example, the rather touching but illustrative case of the Jamaican bus conductor who, in Britain, felt free to date a nurse from his own country – something that would have created all sorts of difficulties in the society he had left, where 'a bus conductor . . . dating a State Registered Nurse might be the talk of the town'.

These distinctions are of vital significance in understanding the response of older black people to racial and class disadvantage in Britain. It was not as though they came from a cohesive folk society in which everyone shared a common poverty, or coped in a co-operative or equal way with adversities. Far from it: the social barriers of British society in the days of full employment, though formidable and unjust, were usually no worse, for migrants from poorer backgrounds, than the race and class barriers of the old country.

It should also be remembered that as a rule age does *not* significantly alter status in the West Indies (see Chapter 2). As Foner (1973: 29) concludes: 'The old men respected in the community are those who have been financially successful, leaders in the churches and voluntary associations, and substantial landowners'. And though she also points out that a lowered, dependent status 'is more true of elderly men than women, since older women can still act in useful roles such as caring for grandchildren', such valued domestic roles are hardly likely to make much difference to the class position of older women in the Caribbean.

Life in Britain – a 'taste of honey'?

In Britain in 1961 a rather gloomy 'kitchen sink realist' film entitled *A Taste of Honey* was released. It was based on an earlier stage play (Delaney 1959) in which, incidentally, a black seaman from Cardiff begins the action in a brief liaison with a rootless white girl.

A 'taste of honey' seems to capture the experience of a great many of the Caribbean migrants to Britain: brief expectation and hope followed by a much longer period of coming to terms with a rather grey British reality. The beginnings of disillusion are apparent in books written about the early days of Afro-Caribbean settlement in London (Little 1947; Patterson 1965). Patterson presents graphic case studies of the men's and women's struggles to find accommodation and jobs, and it is striking that most had, at that time, ideas of a relatively brief stay in Britain. Yet, of all the cases examined, only one couple managed to return to Jamaica according to their plan, within a year or so (Patterson 1965: 277).

The Britain to which most of the older black Afro-Caribbeans came was a society still much constrained by early post-war stuffiness and notions of respectability, but veering towards rather profound cultural changes. It was a society in which it was still legal to discriminate openly against black people applying for jobs or a place to live. It was also a country which had adopted an officially *laissez-faire* policy towards the settlement of black people – migrants were not helped or officially guided towards places of work (unless they were in the minority who had been directly recruited) and there were no organized or state-run attempts to provide or reserve housing.

As a result, and as well portrayed in other studies of the immigration period (for example, by Rex and Moore 1967), most of the newly arrived found themselves lodging with fellow West Indians, usually in cramped, poor and sometimes unhealthy accommodation. With the arrival of greater numbers of

women from the Caribbean, life took on a more settled pattern than before
(Patterson 1965; Foner 1979). In the bigger communities in London,
Birmingham and Manchester, clubs and associations were formed – recreational clubs for drinking and dancing, cricket and dominoes; co-operative
saving associations; and churches or religious associations for both established
denominations and evangelical groups.

Yet, for all the significance of such 'ethnic' associations in the early days, the
impression given by studies of Caribbean people of the time is also of a group
trying to 'fit' into British society – wanting to mix with the white majority and
willing to adapt in various ways. A strong consciousness of 'respectability'
comes across in the accounts of both Little and Patterson, showing that native
white British norms were rather stricter in those days, but also that the black
newcomers were very anxious to establish their respectability; for example,
Patterson (1965: 283) mentions the case of the unmarried mother who 'wears
a wedding ring and calls herself "Mrs" K at the request of the landlord, who
thinks it more respectable'.

The migrants of the 1950s and 1960s not only had to deal with outright
racism but were often – not always – meeting with reserve and a lack of
sociability among the local white population (Patterson 1965: 247). Inter-
racial marriages and other relationships did begin at this time, and have
proportionately increased so that today very substantial numbers of younger
Afro-Caribbeans marry white partners (Nanton 1992). However, it was
common to experience social distance in those days. As Patterson noted, it was
one thing for West Indians to visit the same pubs as white people or to work in
the same factories, but another to find a white person who would invite them
home or establish friendship.

In the period of peak migration to Britain, before 1962, demand for labour
was high and there was almost full (male) employment. As we pointed out in
Chapter 2, Afro-Caribbean migrants were not as a complete group forced into
an 'underclass' position in the labour market. However, as Peach (1991: 26)
shows, the Caribbeans' experiences of work opportunities in Britain has been
an 'Irish' one – that is, they have played much the same role as Irish migrants in
providing a replacement workforce for native white British people, many of
whom experienced a degree of upward social mobility in the 1950s and 1960s.
The Afro-Caribbean community included significant proportions of skilled
men and qualified women, such as nurses, who tended to be employed either
in large-scale public sector organizations (such as transport and health
services) or in 'traditional' industries.

The history of this is important because, as Peach points out, public sector
organizations and heavy industries (for example, engineering and car manufacturing in the Midlands) have been especially prone to 'shake-outs',
redundancy or 'rationalization'. Add to this the slowing down of economic
growth in the 1960s and 1970s, together with the phenomenal rise of
unemployment in the 1980s, and it is perhaps no wonder that a more recent
book about Afro-Caribbeans (in Britain and the Netherlands) was titled *Lost
Illusions* (Cross and Entzinger 1988).

A final aspect of disillusion is the failure of race relations to improve in
Britain. This is not to deny that many Afro-Caribbeans have accommodated

Preparing for the big step – the early 1960s
Photograph: Dyche Collection

themselves to the constraints of British life. Being disillusioned does not necessarily mean complete unhappiness; it is possible to adjust to more modest hopes than one had on arrival. And some, at least, have had more than one taste of honey, as the individual cases below show. However, some of the memories of how they were treated in the early years of settlement in Britain do not fade from older black people's minds – indeed, expectations of racial prejudice may well resurface to affect attitudes to 'white' social services (see Chapter 8).

Above all, a sense of lack of improvement in race relations is heightened by worries about the younger generation. Inner-city riots or 'urban disturbances', as they are euphemistically called, are only the flashpoints in a long, smouldering period of discontent among considerable numbers of younger black people. They worry the older migrant generation, not just because disorder is unsettling or threatening in itself, but because the frustration and anger expressed by the young raise deeper questions about what black people have been able to achieve in British society.

Going 'home'?

Taking stock of the British experience, the decision of some to return to the Caribbean is therefore understandable. In Chapter 2 we briefly touched on this and in Chapter 4 noted that, compared with older Asian people, the Afro-Caribbeans appear to be the more dissatisfied with British life and more often to show signs of wishing to live in another country.

Peach (1991: 12), comparing census totals of people born in the Caribbean over the past three decades, is convinced that return migration is a growing phenomenon. If he is right, it will have serious implications. If substantial numbers are returning 'home' when they reach retirement age, it will probably be even more difficult than before to arouse official interest in the welfare and health needs of older black people, even though a majority might stay to eventually die in Britain. Return migration among the migrant cohorts of Afro-Caribbeans would mean that they would fit much more the European *Gastarbeiter* model than that of an established, if marginalized, minority.

The questions about return migration raised by Peach are based on a comparison of the 1966 total of the Caribbean-born population (330,000) with a 1986–8 total of 233,000. He makes the point that 'the figures are by no means certain since they depend on sample surveys', but if we accept some uncertainty and trust the totals, they suggest 'a decrease of about 97,000 over a twenty-two year period or a loss of 4,400 per year' (Peach 1991: 12).

Referring to evidence on death rates, Peach shows that only a small proportion of the apparent shrinkage of the Caribbean-born population can be accounted for by death; the rest (an estimated 86,000 people over the period) are presumed to have left Britain. Nearly all these will have been migrants born in the Caribbean, though Peach does mention the possibility that a small proportion leaving the United Kingdom are not returnees but British-born, Caribbean-descent children of the migrants.

Apart from the uncertainties of the sample figures on which Peach's estimations are based, however, there is a much bigger question mark against the rate or scale of return migration, as Peach himself points out. This is because there appears to be yet little trace of the returned migrants in any of the Caribbean islands or a third country such as Canada. They have 'vanished'. The supposed numbers are not inconsiderable: Peach estimates that 48,000, for example, would have returned to Jamaica – yet one sees no significant official or public comment on this in the Caribbean.

The question of return migration is still an open one, therefore. It is likely that we may have to revise the assumptions made in the community surveys (for example, Bhalla and Blakemore 1981; Barker 1984) that return migration would be minimal. The largest cohort of Afro-Caribbeans is only now reaching retirement, so assuming a significant group postpone return until they are in their early sixties, we may yet see more definite signs of return in the Caribbean itself.

There is another possibility, not considered by Peach: that inaccuracies in the British figures are the result not just of sampling errors, but of a much more widespread avoidance of census enumeration in the Afro-Caribbean community. In other words, at least some of the 'missing 86,000' may not have returned to the Caribbean at all. We suggest this because the experience of fieldwork for the AFFOR study in Birmingham, for example, seemed to reveal significantly more older black people 'on the ground' than expected from the 1981 Census or mid-1970s estimates (Bhalla and Blakemore 1981). Alienation from many aspects of officialdom is very high in such areas as Handsworth and Lozells in Birmingham, and personal impressions based on fieldwork in these areas suggest that it can be quite difficult to win people over to the idea of being interviewed or even contacted; single older black people sharing a house with others, perhaps living in one or two rooms, can in our experience be easily missed.

Personal experience in context

We will now examine the personal experiences of older Afro-Caribbean people, interviewed in the Midlands and elsewhere, in the light of the 'background' observations made above. As will be seen, the individuals who have told us about their lives illustrate broad historical trends, such as rising unemployment and changing community relations in Britain. However, the value of individual cases goes beyond this. Sometimes an individual's experience contradicts the trend, suggesting a variety of responses to ageing or coping with life in Britain.

It may be useful to bear in mind the images of 'self-reliant pioneer', 'gradually adjusting migrant' and 'passive victim' as one way of trying to understand these different responses, though in the conclusion we will qualify the use of such categories.

'Why am I here?' – Arrival, work and neighbourhood

As we mentioned, most older Afro-Caribbean people came to Britain in the 1950s and early 1960s, though a few came later and a very few earlier. In

Birmingham in the early 1980s, we found that almost two-thirds of the men but only two-fifths of the women had lived in Britain for 20 years or more. The women tended to arrive a few years after the men, though the overwhelming majority of men and women had lived in Britain for 11 years or more at that time (Bhalla and Blakemore 1981).

A large proportion of the older black people interviewed then, and in a 'follow-up' survey (Blakemore 1984), had come to Britain in middle age. Those who arrived when they were younger, in their twenties or thirties, are the larger cohorts due to reach retirement age in the 1990s. Until then, we are mainly dealing with those who arrived in their forties, fifties and even in their early sixties.

For example, Miss A did domestic work in Monserrat until she came to Britain in 1966, at the age of 58, to live with her son and grandchildren. Mrs C sold children's clothes and worked as a domestic help in a hospital in Jamaica until 1967, when she came to Britain at the age of 48 to work in hospital catering. Mr G did not arrive in Britain until he was 49. He had worked as a baker, but arriving in 1961 he took a series of unskilled jobs in engineering and car manufacturing. An interesting exception was Mr H, who arrived in Britain in 1929 at the age of 23, worked in a brewery in Burton-on-Trent until 1972, and then retired to Birmingham. He is an example of a 'pioneer' migrant in the pre-1940s sense referred to by Barker (1984: 19) and is almost alone in this respect in the AFFOR sample.

Arriving as many did in middle age and with what seem to have been modest work expectations, it is not surprising that the sense of frustration one may discover among younger black people (Pryce 1986) is not so apparent in this age group. Most of the older migrants have been in semi-skilled work and have usually changed jobs only two or three times since arrival, though this could suggest a degree of racial discrimination in employment as much as satisfaction with employment. For women, semi-skilled factory work is quite frequently mentioned, but working for a public sector employer – usually as a cook, cleaner or ancillary worker – had been the most common experience. Among the men, factory work had predominated (Bhalla and Blakemore 1981; Blakemore 1984).

Longer 'biographical' interviews revealed that in many cases migrants had been unable to apply their previously learned skills to work in Britain. This was not true of the women who had worked as cooks or cleaners in the West Indies and continued to do so in Britain. But even in these cases there were women who had previously combined such work in the Caribbean with other activities such as 'higglering' or trading, or working as seamstresses, which they were not able to keep up after arrival.

The older men also experienced considerable discontinuity in work experience, typically exchanging farming or trading in the West Indies for factory work in Britain. A strong interest in gardening and growing vegetables, readily observable in some of the older men, is no doubt a reflection of their rural backgrounds.

In a few cases it was possible for skills learned in the West Indies to be transferred. Despite the pressures to keep black workers in relatively unskilled jobs, apparent in the following example, the case of Mr P is illustrative. Mr P described the day in 1956 when he started work at the Post Office, 12 days after his arrival in Britain:

> The Labour Office sent me off as a cleaner to the Post Office. When the foreman come at nine o'clock, I tell him really this is not my line, I'm a cabinet maker. It's my trade . . . He wanted to give me a trial. He gave me bus fare and I went and fetched the tools back, from the flat. He goin' to give me a test – a dovetail and another job. It was very good . . . clean it off, ready for polish. After passin' that test . . . [*laughs*] . . . He said, 'You put me in trouble . . . the union can't allow to return me back to bein' a cleaner! . . . So I go from department to department . . . Okay, so after a week they squeeze me into a little space [in a carpenters' workshop] . . . they say they give me a month's trial. Well, I did one month, everything quite satisfactory. I stayed there twenty two years till I retire.
>
> Mr P

Discrimination is apparent in this account in the way Mr P was deemed fit only for unskilled work by the Labour Exchange, and perhaps in the run-around he received as a result of the union demarcation of trades – a less determined person might have given up. On the other hand, encouragement and tolerance are also apparent, as was the pride of this man in his reliability and the work he had done. Mr P's initial persistence and continuing self-confidence illustrate aspects of the 'self-reliant pioneer' image. However, as an example of transferring skills from the Caribbean he is rather unusual, at least among the Birmingham sample.

Neighbourhood

Older Afro-Caribbeans have experienced, as Barker (1984: 20) comments, 'a remarkable stability of living arrangements and locality of residence'. Barker's study was of Manchester and London, though the same is true of Birmingham and other cities with Caribbean communities, such as Bristol.

In Birmingham 65 per cent of the men and 57 per cent of the women had lived in their present neighbourhood for 16 years or more (Bhalla and Blakemore 1981). Residence is particularly stable in the established areas of Caribbean settlement such as Handsworth or Soho, though less so in other Birmingham wards.

As with employment, housing stability is as much a sign of racial discrimination in the housing market as an expression of choice. There is not much evidence that older Caribbean residents are very happy with their neighbourhoods, as some of the cases below illustrate. However, staying put has resulted in a degree of identification with, and rootedness in, local neighbourhoods. Older Afro-Caribbeans are almost as well-established in their neighbourhoods as the older white residents. They often share with older whites attitudes towards the behaviour of younger people, a perceived loss of 'friendly' neighbourhoods and the degradation of the physical environment. In this sense the image of 'gradually adjusting migrant' is quite appropriate because many have identified with their neighbourhoods.

Contrasting with these present-day views are some interesting and generally positive memories of city neighbourhoods as they were when the older respondents arrived:

> I came to Balsall Heath first. It was nice, you could go an' visit friends, come back at any time. Not like now – I'm afraid to go out on my own.
>
> Mrs E

> Handsworth was beautiful then. You could walk in the area at any time of day or night. We had good neighbours, white and black. There were good shops.
>
> Mrs B

> Livin' conditions were a bit rough. It was a surprise. Livin' in one room wasn't to me suit, you know. But whatever part of the world, some is alright and some is a bit rough. Livin' here was okay.
>
> Mr N

Not all the memories of the neighbourhood on arrival were positive or at least basically satisfied, however. Though there was no mention of explicit racial hostility or violence in these early days, it seemed clear that some had moved away from neighbourhoods they did not feel welcome in. The image of 'passive victim' is perhaps too strong in connection with these examples, though there is a feeling of rejection:

> I lived with some relatives in Perry Barr [Birmingham] first. I lived there a year, then moved to Handsworth in 1956. I didn't like Perry Barr. The neighbours weren't friendly. There are much nicer neighbours in Handsworth.
>
> Mrs H

What are we to make of otherwise favourable accounts of what it was like to live in 1950s and early 1960s urban Britain? First, it should be pointed out that the generally favourable quotations refer to the neighbourhood in general. A number of respondents went on to talk about personal difficulties they had experienced finding accommodation or in not settling down in other respects. A second point is that reminiscence tends to elicit rose-tinted views; darker memories are screened out or not mentioned.

Supposing these neighbourhoods *were* more or less as they have been described, older Caribbeans' accounts do tally with the sorts of comments made by older white people who have lived in the same areas for many years (Blakemore 1983c). The economic decline of inner-city areas, rising unemployment and the suburbanization of better-off, younger groups are interconnected factors which have all adversely affected the social fabric of these communities. And though it is possible to make too much of 'loss of community', community ties have declined, as discussed by Fennell *et al.* (1988: 18–24). The older Caribbean migrants caught the beginning of the end of the urban communities of the 1940s and 1950s, when residents knew the names of every household in the street, and almost everyone had grown up in the local area.

Dislike of present-day neighbourhoods is illustrated by the following accounts, though some express dissatisfaction with accommodation (too small or unsuitable, or noisy co-tenants) as much as neighbourhood:

> I don't like this area. The people above me are too noisy. If I had a family in Monserrat, I would be better off there. Here I could die and no one know except the police.
>
> Mrs A

> This place is dirty, full o' rubbish and I get problems with me neighbours. I want to call the Health Inspector.
>
> Mrs D

> It's not like it was. I'm afraid to go out on me own. I'm very frightened after dark.
>
> Mrs E

> Young people have changed. They're unmannerly, no etiquette. They were more decent in the past.
>
> Mr I

Not all the views on the present-day neighbourhood were negative, however, and other comments ranged from indifference to fairly positive comments – a 'gradually adjusting' image again:

> It's quite alright around here. I can go ahead and do just what I want at me own leisure, p'raps go for a pint . . . I just fit meself to me condition. Nothin' worry me, I can adjust meself . . .
>
> Mr P

> I like this area. It's peaceful and I'm lucky to find it. I don't have no trouble, day or night.
>
> Mrs C

> I like my present home now. It's quiet, I got nice neighbours. I wouldn't live in Handsworth now even if they were givin' me a room for nothin'!
>
> Mrs B

Living arrangements and social life

Other studies of the social life of older Afro-Caribbeans (for example, Berry *et al.* 1981; Fenton 1986) give the impression of a mainly dissatisfied, unhappy and lonely group. Fenton's case studies are chosen to illustrate problems of racism and non-acceptance in Britain, feelings of being 'stuck' in a country which holds little promise, and sadness and regret concerning loss of relationships with family.

While these themes also surfaced in our research, we were also struck by the fact that they were not the only ones. Sadness and feelings of isolation exist, but how common are they? Our interviews seemed to suggest a considerably mixed set of responses among older Afro-Caribbean people.

To give some perspective it is worth noting that considerable numbers live alone – over a half of the men and almost a third of the women (AFFOR 1981). But of the rest, just over a third are living with a spouse or partner, while the remainder – about a quarter – are in households of three or more. The Age Concern survey (Barker 1984) showed that similar numbers of Afro-Caribbeans are living alone (37 per cent) or with one other person (31 per cent).

The considerable numbers of older black people living alone should not be considered problems in themselves. Living alone should not be confused with either social isolation or loneliness, which occur independently of living circumstances. Some older people living alone are cheerfully independent. However, it is when living alone combines with other factors, such as chronic illness and dependency, or racial victimization, that it can become a problem. And though they may have relatives scattered far and wide, quite high proportions of older Afro-Caribbeans have no relatives living nearby, or in the same city – about a half of the Birmingham sample, for example.

Older Afro-Caribbean men give particular concern in this respect. Relatively high rates of separation among Afro-Caribbean couples (Foner 1979) mean that some men find themselves relatively isolated in later life; the same may happen to older women, of course, but they are more likely than the men to be in touch with daughters and grandchildren.

Almost a quarter of the older men interviewed in Birmingham were found to be living in rented single rooms. Again, some of these men have active social lives and are reasonably healthy, but it is a sad comment on the general position of a minority of older black men. These men are in some ways continuing a 'self-reliant pioneer' or 'migrant arrival' lifestyle which has been the pattern since their earlier years in Britain. In such cramped and sometimes unhealthy accommodation, their futures seem clouded by vulnerability.

As time passes, however, an increasing proportion of the older Afro-Caribbeans living alone will be women: the migrant population is ageing and, as women tend to outlive men, the proportion of widows will rise. Unfortunately, Afro-Caribbean women appear to be somewhat more socially isolated than the men. Taking the simple measure of going out daily, for example, we found that three-fifths of the Afro-Caribbean men did so, but only two-fifths of the women (AFFOR 1981). Higher rates of chronic illness among the women (see Chapter 7) combined with fear of crime and other negative views about the neighbourhood could account for this. In addition, slightly higher proportions of Afro-Caribbean men see their friends and neighbours every day, compared with the women, though it is the women who have the edge in seeing relatives every day. None of these gender differences in contact with others are particularly sharp, but they do point to a more home-centred life among Afro-Caribbean women.

Gender differences are also apparent in the preferences expressed by older black people in Birmingham about what they like to do (AFFOR 1981). For women, housework and cleaning (40 per cent), sewing, needlework or knitting (31 per cent), reading (15 per cent) and cooking (14 per cent) were the most commonly mentioned activities – but, except for reading, very few of the men mentioned them. They cited watching television, gardening, going out to the pub, shopping or going for a walk as their most preferred activities.

Summing up, it is clear that life in the older Afro-Caribbean community is relatively individuated and home-centred. Many have an extensive network of friends and relatives, but these contacts are often scattered. An increasing number of older black people live alone, and among this group are some very isolated individuals.

Perhaps one exception to this, though in a way confirming the *émigré* identity of the older Afro-Caribbean in Britain, is the place of the church in their spiritual and social lives. Various churches – for example, Seventh Day Adventist, Methodist, Baptist – fulfil distinctive needs and provide a focus for life, especially among the women. According to the Birmingham evidence (AFFOR 1981), two-thirds of older Afro-Caribbeans go to church regularly, a far higher proportion than among the majority community. Most regular attenders go to church once a week, and almost a third of the women visit their churches twice a week or more. Interestingly, these findings differ sharply from Patterson's (1965: 303) discovery that, in the earlier days of migrant settlement (1955–8), 'Most Brixton migrants . . . rarely or never enter a church except for weddings, christenings, and other special occasions'.

This is almost certainly because the Caribbean community then had not had time to establish its own popular churches; also, attendance will probably have risen with age. The following examples of respondents' views illustrate the important role of church and of religion in confirming a sense of Caribbean identity, of providing opportunities for friendship and social activity, as well as strengthening spiritual and psychological reserves in times of illness or loneliness:

> I go to the 'Silver Lining' club every Tuesday [a club run by the Church]. Then I go to the Church Tuesday and Thursday evening, and Sunday morning and evening. I have friends from Church who will help me if I need it, especially in the winter months.
>
> Miss S

> I've got bad legs [from arthritis] and the pain in my side makes doing anything very difficult. But I do go to Church every Saturday. We read the Bible, pray and sing. I haven't done anything specially enjoyable in the last month, but on my birthday everyone at Church came to my house, sang hymns and gave me presents.
>
> Mrs A

Though a substantial proportion of men attend a church regularly, church life and religion seem to occupy a less central place for them. Some older men have settled into a relatively disengaged but contented life. There are strong elements of the 'adjusted migrant' in these men's accounts:

> I been here so long, I become a stranger to the people in Jamaica. Most o' me friends have died. Me meself, I'm very comfortable here. I would never, not for one minute, give this country a bad name. I don't have a special routine for any day, not even Sunday. I'm very happy with what I'm doin' now. Here I've got me garden and I occupy meself. The neighbours would give me any land, if I needed it.
>
> Mr I

> I definitely can go out and enjoy meself when I want to. But usually, well I do housework, go to shop, cook a little food. On Sundays I get up a little

What is the future for older Afro-Caribbean people?
Photograph: Abdullah Badwi

early, do Sunday dinner, watch T.V. . . . My two sons don't live here now. They comes round often.

Mr N

Though most of the women contacted in the 'follow-up' survey (Blakemore 1984) felt they would be better off in the West Indies as far as social life and supportive relationships are concerned, a few seemed relatively content with a limited if somewhat disengaged life in Britain. More common among the women, however, were feelings of unhappiness with a disengaged and lonely existence, though we should not forget those with active and full social lives. Typical of those who expressed regret about their lives in Britain were the following:

I would like to go home to Jamaica, but there's no one there now. I have no money. In the day I do my own housework, shopping . . . I could do a lot more, if there was more to do.

Mrs J

I'm better off in England money-wise. There's no social security in Jamaica. But family ties are better in Jamaica. I got four brothers and two sisters there. I cooks, cleans . . . nothin' special to do in the daytime.

Mrs A

Again and again, illness plays a significant part in limiting the social lives and activities of a substantial proportion of the women:

I miss all my family in St Kitts. If my own children were in St Kitts I'd prefer to be there. My sons an' daughter visit but they've got their own lives to lead [in Yorkshire]. I used to go to day classes, sewing . . . adult education. But my illness [diabetes, arthritis, stiffness and sore feet] stop that.

Mrs Y

I'd like to do more but me illnesses hold me back. The blood pressure is very bad, I dare not do any outside work. The diabetes is not too bad at all now, but the arthritis stop me walkin' too far. My husband is not too well himself. Luckily we're not usually ill at the same time.

Mrs M

The latter account underlines the need for social or day centres for some Afro-Caribbean people (see Chapter 8). As the migrant generation ages, the numbers in this category are rising sharply. The Caribbean community has many strengths, not least the extended and interconnected networks of family and friends which are rooted in the island communities from which they came. However, for some older people these ties have been weakened or lost altogether – as some of the above accounts show. When such relatively isolated people become chronically ill, the presence of a nearby day centre which can offer Caribbean food, some social contact and an understanding welcome becomes doubly important.

Age and ageing

We have already mentioned that, according to Foner (1973; 1979), older people in Caribbean society are normally accorded respect but that old age does not in itself confer authority or high status. However, our respondents were of the opinion that *in comparison with Britain* the position of older people in the Caribbean is still significantly more favourable:

I didn't fear growing old in St Kitts. Older people are more respected and cared for than here.

Mrs Y

Since my husband's retirement I've really enjoyed myself here. We had a real good party when he retire. But I did look forward to retirin' in Jamaica. Old people are better cared for there.

Mrs B

While some of these images are sustained by memories of a past era, there are those who recognise changes in Caribbean society, as this comment on recollections of a recent visit to Jamaica shows:

We were told by our mother to help old people if we saw them, to carry their bags, to see them to their doors. My mother would cook food and send it over the road to an elderly neighbour. But today it is different there, not like before.

Miss H

There were also differences of opinion in discussions of the meaning of 'old age' or 'old person'. Some emphasized the continuity between mid-life and later life in Caribbean society, as opposed to the rather sharp categorization of old age in Britain, with the onset of retirement:

Old age and retirement is not an issue in Jamaica. You just work until you feel you want to stop. I never think about old age as such.

Mrs F

I didn't even consider such a thing as old age back home. And I don't think about it now.

Mrs M

In the above responses there is an element of carrying on regardless of age categorization. A rather different attitude was apparent among others, however, and may be typified as a stoic acceptance of old age. Expectations of happiness or successful ageing are low. Old age is seen as nearness to death rather than as a new phase of life. But though there is sadness, regret and some passivity, feelings are balanced by religious and philosophical acceptance:

I'm not frightened. I thanks God and takes each day as it comes. I feel lucky to have reached this age [63].

Mrs C

I did want to reach this age [71] as my grandmother lived to be 100 and my mother until 84. But I'm just grateful for each birthday, nothing more. I look forward to it . . . all the family get together an' visit me . . .

Miss S

Finally, there were expressions of a more dissatisfied, even bitter, attitude towards old age. These responses were often linked with chronic illness, loneliness, or feelings of being unwanted in Britain. These feelings should not necessarily be associated with a set group of older Afro-Caribbean people, as in changed circumstances some of the respondents above may also share such perceptions:

I didn't think I'd be on me own at this age. I feels lonely an' get depressed . . . the T.V. is me only company.

Mrs D

Britain is too cold . . . I have me friend from America here now but she goes back soon – I'll really miss her . . . I thought about getting old when I was young but I didn't fear it. But when me husband died . . . I fear death, it showed me how near death is to life and how easy it is to die . . .

Mrs A

I suffer from serious diabetes and I go into comas sometimes. I'm losing weight and my hands tremble. I feel depressed, run down . . .

Mrs Y

Conclusion

The aim of this chapter was to try to capture the essence of the Afro-Caribbean experience of growing old in Britain. But, as the variety of their comments and observations has shown, this essence is something of an illusion. There are those who are burdened by money worries, while others have the resources to consider a visit or a return to the West Indies; some see hardly anyone for days but others have busy social lives; some are trapped by chronic illness, others are not; and while some openly express feelings of bitterness and regret, others either stoically downplay such feelings or express satisfaction with life in Britain.

For these reasons it is difficult to say with any statistical certainty how many Afro-Caribbean people are ageing successfully, or are either basically satisfied or dissatisfied. We should also remember the fragility of any older person's circumstances. For anyone, the death of a spouse or valued friend, or the onset of serious illness, or the departure of a son or daughter may bring sudden and significant change. For those older migrants who do not have a close-knit support network, any one of these changes will expose the precariousness and vulnerability of their position. It can therefore be misleading to be too definite about the proportions who are experiencing a problematic old age as opposed to those who are not.

The impression that all or most older Afro-Caribbeans experience sharp problems of deprivation, neglect, worry and regret, conveyed by previous studies, is not borne out. There are significant problems and needs among *some*, but Rowland's conclusion that there has been too much concern with social problems and a 'negative bias in research' (Rowland 1991: 59) on minority ageing seems to apply to the Afro-Caribbean case.

Once we are clear that there are different responses or sets of experiences among older black people, it becomes a little easier to begin the task of identifying them. In our discussion of case studies, we attempted to show how the three images of ageing – the 'self-reliant pioneer', the 'gradually adjusting migrant' and the 'passive victim' – did throw some light on individual experiences. But as we previously pointed out, these images may lead to stereotypes.

Other differences between groups of older Afro-Caribbeans are discernible. At one end of a spectrum, there are individuals who are definitely experiencing a problematic old age and who consciously express feelings about this. They are beset with problems: chronic illness plays a significant part, especially among the women, but there are other problems of poverty, inadequate accommodation and social isolation. And there is an overlay of memories of racism, often combined with dashed hopes and regrets about staying in Britain. We could term this group 'the marooned'.

At the other end of the spectrum are those who are ageing successfully: they are socially engaged, having active and satisfying social lives, and expressing satisfaction with their position. For those in this group, there is a network of Caribbean community organizations, clubs and churches in all the major British cities, though they are also likely to have contacts with white majority people in mixed-race settings: a wedding, a party, or a pub.

Though the evidence on return migration is inconclusive, it is possible that potential returnees are most likely to be among this group. This might seem paradoxical, as they would appear to be the most settled. However, they are also the people who have escaped poverty, and many have social ties and other resources in the West Indies to facilitate a successful return. We stress that this is a speculative point, and we are not saying that all such older people are likely to return – they are part 'self-reliant pioneers' and part 'adjusted migrants' and, if the 'adjusted' aspect of their experience is the more important to them, they will perhaps be content to stay in Britain.

The remainder of older Afro-Caribbeans appear to be divided into two other groups. First, there are those whose circumstances seem to be as problematic as among the first group. However, they could be described as a 'problematic ageing, accepting' group. Not a few respondents displayed attitudes of stoicism and of religious or philosophical acceptance of the difficulties they faced. As with older white people, low expectations and an unwillingness to place demands on the health services can lead to a kind of collusion between practitioners and those in need – an assumption that 'there isn't really a problem' and that not much could be done even if problems were brought into the open.

Finally, there is a group who lead unproblematic and rather quiet, home-centred lives. Unlike the actively engaged second group, these older people have contact with a relatively narrow range of others: a spouse or partner, a few friends, occasional contact with other members of a church or club. Some might occasionally become more socially engaged than they usually are – during a flurry of family celebrations, for example. If unburdened by health worries and if they have more meaningful relationships with people in the West Indies than in Britain, then we might expect that some of this group will also become return migrants.

6

The Asians' experiences

Introduction – a shared past

The personal histories of older people of Asian backgrounds, and the social histories of their communities, are intertwined with British history, and especially with Britain's colonial past. At the time of writing, someone who grew up in India or Pakistan and is aged 65 will have been in their twenty-first year at the time of India's independence (1947) and only a little older during the momentous and terrible events following the Partition of India and Pakistan. This is just one illustration of the many changes which are woven into the past of older Asian people now living in Britain.

To the historical events and changes which happened in the old country we must add the significant social changes they have experienced in Britain since the 1960s: for example, the decline of traditional industries and the emergence of a 'rust belt' in parts of the North of England, West Midlands and South Wales; the destruction or 'redevelopment' of many inner-city areas; the rise of unemployment; new social attitudes to leisure and 'consumerism'; and new forms of social conflict, including elements of racism and protests about black immigration from political opinion on the right.

We are starting with these observations because many in the white majority, including practitioners and welfare professionals, fail to see Asian communities and Asian individuals as part of this past, or as people who share present-day concerns with them; but Asians, too, are concerned about mortgage interest rates, finding the right school for their children, finding a job, making wedding arrangements for sons or daughters.

Also, the cultures and societies of the Indian subcontinent have had, and will continue to have, a tremendous influence on British society; the presence in Britain of ageing Asian migrants and their descendants is but one aspect of this. Conversely, life in India, Pakistan or Bangladesh is still influenced by Britain –

not only as a result of the dwindling colonial legacy, but also by present-day English language media of communication and by commercial ties. This is particularly evident in the relatively few Indian, Pakistani and Bangladeshi regions or districts from which migrants to Britain have come. For example, in some villages in the Punjab one might suddenly see a group of children in Marks and Spencer cardigans or summerwear – gifts from relatives living in Britain. Land, houses and agricultural purchases are often funded by re-mittances from British Asian workers.

Though British television, radio and newspapers give relatively little coverage of the preoccupations and concerns of Asian people, either in Britain or on the Indian subcontinent (unless there is a major political crisis overseas, or a racial conflict in Britain), there is at least some attention to Asian matters in the 'quality' press and occasionally in television or radio documentaries. For practitioners in the health and social service fields, there is a growing number of texts and training manuals which provide information on the social and cultural background of the various Asian communities (for example, Baxter *et al.* 1986; Henley and Taylor 1986). There is also a large and growing academic literature on the cultures and changing circumstances of British Asian communities (Dhanjal 1976; Jeffery 1976; Saifullah Khan 1976; Anwar 1979; Bhachu 1985; Shaw 1988; Werbner 1989; Stopes-Roe and Cochrane 1990).

But despite the bonds between Britain and Asia, and despite the availability of information, one has the impression that many in the 'caring' professions – let alone the general public – are, if not openly prejudiced in their attitudes towards Asian people and communities, either uninterested or uninformed. This is shown quite well by a recent survey of white British people's attitudes towards arranged marriages in Asian communities. It was found that the majority do not approve of arranged marriage, and that 'in spite of some efforts towards tolerance . . . the British attitude . . . is generally uncomprehending where it is not hostile' (Stopes-Roe and Cochrane 1990: 44).

The prospects for a wider understanding of the needs of older Asian people, their personal experiences and cultural contexts, are therefore clouded by a history of social distance, indifference and coolness, if not hostility among the white majority. Asian people's social lives and priorities are often seen as 'too different' from majority norms, incomprehensible and insufficiently adapted. And their religious beliefs and cultural practices are typified as barbaric in comparison with Western values, leading to views of Asian cultures as pathological sources of social problems or mental distress.

Are these misapprehensions entirely the responsibility of the majority? As we suggested in Chapter 3, all the British Asian communities can be seen to a greater or lesser extent as 'immigrant' minorities still. That is, the preoccu-pations, values and standards of many British Asians – especially the older generation – are shaped more by the culture of the old country than by British or Western influences. The causes of this lie not simply in cultural conservatism or concerns with one's own ethnic group than in the *relationship* which has developed between the white majority and the Asian minorities. As Shaw reminds us, the early migrants to Britain found themselves in a relatively hostile or unwelcoming society. Their 'initial dependence on each other for work, accommodation and welfare had the generally conservative effect of ensuring that migrants acted according to their original purpose and cultural values' (1988: 49).

The young and middle-aged women who joined these migrants – those women now approaching old age – had little opportunity to learn English or to meet white neighbours or workmates. This is not to say that a large proportion wanted to do these things or should necessarily be expected to do so, but even where some Asian women did wish to learn English they were often discouraged or even forbidden from doing so, especially in the Pakistani community (Jeffery 1976).

Before considering examples of the personal experiences of older Asian people, it therefore seems important to explore in a little more detail these facets of the older Asians' backgrounds. What social changes and social aspects of the Asian communities in Britain are affecting their old age? We suggest that two major themes have dominated life in all the Asian communities, affecting older people as much as anyone else: first, the changing nature of family and kinship ties, and second, the particular importance of gender divisions and distinctions in Asian communities. These two themes find different expression in the different Asian communities and, where appropriate, we will try to highlight exceptions and distinctive patterns.

Changing family and kinship ties

None of the substantial number of studies of Britain's various Asian communities explicitly discusses the role of older people. Usually it is only by inference that we are able to learn anything from these studies about ageing and relationships between the generations. Stopes-Roe and Cochrane's (1990) book, for example, has a full discussion of inter-generational ties but is in the main concerned with relations between the young and the middle-aged. To take another example, Werbner's (1989) study of British Pakistanis provides a detailed anthropology of marriage, kinship and gift or exchange relationships, but older people are not discussed as a social category or group.

However, it is clear from these studies that Asian communities have undergone a steady accumulation of changes, some small and some great, in family life. Despite the persistence of cultural conservatism and family ties with the old country, no Asian community can remain in a completely static position. As we discussed above (see Chapter 3), it is still an open question as to whether some Asian communities will, through social mobility, leave behind their 'immigrant' status to achieve the position of 'autonomous' minorities. It is also possible that some Asian people of the third and fourth generations will not find much enhancement of their social position or, even worse, will be indefinitely marginalized in a 'caste-like' status.

All these possibilities of social change have major implications for the status and position of older people. Some close observers of Asian communities in Britain (for example, Randhawa 1993) are convinced that family roles, values and responsibilities are on the brink of major change: the first significant group of British-born Asians (those born in the late 1960s and 1970s) have now 'come of age' and are rearing their own children; associated with these developments have come revised attitudes towards the extended family, which Randhawa believes are demonstrated by a less caring view of older people and a greater preparedness among the British-born adults to reject close ties with them. How much evidence is there, to date, that changing family circumstances are seriously affecting the status of older Asian people?

Werbner (1989: 32) found that a degree of social mobility among some of the Pakistani families in her Manchester study had resulted in residential scattering of the families and a trend towards living in smaller households. Though she does not comment on the impact this may be having on older people, there is a danger of feelings of isolation among the older relatives. Cantor (1976), in a study of Mexican Americans in the United States, found that *perceived* threats to traditional family supports were sufficient to cause relatively high levels of anxiety, depression and feelings of loneliness among older members of this group – even though, objectively, the Mexican American elderly group were the best supported in terms of living with relatives or receiving help, visits and social contact. If the position of older Asians in Britain is analogous to that of the Mexican Americans, we might conclude that even relatively slight changes to family and residential patterns could lead to the identification of this as a very serious problem by the older Asian people.

While this is conjecture, other research has shown definite evidence of the marginalization of older people in families. In Leamington Spa, for example, a surprisingly high number of problems stemming from isolation and loneliness were discovered in a small group of older Sikh women who, upon initial contact, appeared to be well integrated in supportive family networks (Boneham 1989). Five of the twenty were found to be not living in the extended family, rather preferring to live independently as widows or couples. Others were unhappy, though living with sons and their families, were frequently left alone and living some distance from the *gurdwara* and Asian friends. They had moved with sons who were 'aspiring middle class' and were left isolated on predominantly white suburban residential estates. Discouraged from meeting out of doors in Britain either because of social norms affecting women or the adverse climate, these older people spoke of feelings of incarceration, loneliness and abandonment. The case of Mrs Bajunder is illustrative:

> She spoke no English and was completely dependent on family support . . . she was anxious, isolated and frustrated. She cried 'no one has time for us'. Her grandchildren did not talk to her because of their lack of Punjabi. Her son and daughter-in-law were at work all day. Her son had no car and was not showing them the country he had promised in his letters. Her passport had been taken by her son, and she feared he was trying to get her settled here when she really just wanted to go back to India. On one occasion she wept 'I want to run out of this house. I do not want to stay a minute more.'
>
> (Boneham 1989: 454)

Evidence from another study (Blakemore 1984) also showed that relatively few older Asian women seemed to be enjoying the kinds of social activity cited by Werner, Bhachu and others, such as making preparations for weddings, getting involved in religious duties at the temple or *gurdwara*, or simply visiting other kin and friends. Possibly some older women are being left out of the arrangements made by the younger British-born generation, though further study is needed to test this assumption.

Among older men there are certainly signs of 'marginalization' from time to time. All the main community surveys have shown, for example, that older Asian men quite frequently mention aimless wandering in the street, which is certainly a form of freedom not open to women, visiting parks or chatting to acquaintances as ways of passing the time. Though a good deal of this reflects cultural preference, mirroring the kind of open-air socializing among the men of the community in India or Pakistan, there is also an element of rejection and marginalization, especially when the weather is too cold for leisurely chatting on the street. As Harlan (1964) showed in a much earlier study of inter-generational relationships in village communities in India, older men and women are not always wanted around the home or involving themselves in younger people's conversations (see Chapter 3).

To keep this in perspective, however, we must remember that a large proportion of older Asian people continue to live with their relatives in large households. This is not just a matter of convenience or custom, but of strongly valued attachment to family unity in many cases. In studies of Asians' attitudes – admittedly, in Jeffery's case, almost twenty years ago – both the high rate of divorce among whites and an apparent neglect of older family members are frequently cited as the drawbacks or moral failings of Western lifestyles (Jeffery 1976: 95). Despite a degree of conflict to be expected in any domestic group, family life in most Asian homes is warm, convivial and supportive. By way of illustration, we might consider Shaw's (1988) study of a Pakistani community, which shows how, as in Pakistan, a home is completely shared: 'no individual or couple regards a room as their own' and 'each room is everyone's' (1988: 61). These particular observations cannot be generalized to all Asian communities, but they do illustrate strong beliefs in interdependence and solidarity.

The evidence from the community surveys on residence patterns seems to uphold the idea of a fairly resilient extended family or of joint family households which include the oldest members. The Age Concern survey showed that 71 per cent of their sample lived in households of six or more people (Barker 1984: 22); the equivalent proportion in Birmingham (61 per cent) was also quite high (Bhalla and Blakemore 1981).

In other towns and cities, though, patterns of residence are different and show that notions of older Asian people living in large households can be far from the norm. In Coventry, only a quarter of over 1,100 older Asian people were found to be living in households of six or more (see Table 6.1).

The explanation for this lies partly in differences in housing stock in the two cities. Coventry has a much smaller stock of older properties in its inner ring as a result of wartime destruction and post-war 'redevelopment'; Birmingham, on the other hand, has a larger stock of older and bigger houses and – despite long-standing housing problems among immigrants (Rex and Moore 1967) – this has permitted the establishment of larger Asian households. The differences between the two cities may therefore provide lessons for other urban areas and highlight the continued need for larger sizes of house in inner-city areas.

Table 6.1   Size of household of older Asians aged 55 and
over in Birmingham and Coventry

Number in household	Coventry[1] (per cent)	Birmingham[2] (per cent)
Living alone	3	5
2	17	10
3–5	54	24
6+	26	61
Total	100	100
N	1,163	169

[1] Coventry (1986)
[2] AFFOR (1981)

Further comparisons between Birmingham and Coventry Asian communities show that while each city has roughly the same proportions of major ethno-religious groups – Punjabi Sikhs (about half) and Gujarati-speaking Hindus (about a quarter) – over a quarter of Coventry's older Asians have come from East African countries, whereas all but a few of those in Birmingham come directly from the Indian subcontinent.

Bhachu's (1985: 63) study of the East African Asian settlers shows that they are much more likely than the other Asian communities to live in nuclear family groups than in joint households. She identifies not only this trend, but also a number of other changes in family life: the growing control by women over their own marriage arrangements and choice of partner, for example, and a trend towards younger couples setting up home on their own. It is therefore very likely that Coventry – along with Leicester, some Asian communities in south London and elsewhere – exhibits at least in part the 'East African' effect discussed above, and illustrates how in such communities increasing numbers of grandparents and senior relatives will be living with couples, on their own, or most likely with two or three younger relatives (a son and daughter-in-law, for example). Interestingly, this pattern has already occurred among Sikhs in a British Columbian community, though, it will be recalled, not necessarily as a result of 'modernizing' influences (see Chapter 3).

Changing ideas about living in smaller households are also becoming evident in 'direct migrant' Asian families in all the major ethnic communities, according to Stopes-Roe and Cochrane. They found that, in the West Midlands, 'a third of all fathers and 40 per cent of the mothers said they would prefer to live in a nuclear family' (1990: 70). This is an aspiration rather than intention, and it is not based on responses from older people. Also, despite changing attitudes, the proportion of older Asians living alone or even in couples remains very low. So despite growing signs of change in household structure and in attitudes to family, a key difference between older Asian people, on the whole, and either Afro-Caribbean or white older people is still the relative rarity among older Asians of living alone or in couples.

Two notes of caution need to be sounded, however. The first is that a much larger proportion of older Asian people than those actually living alone seem to *perceive* their position as one of being alone. This is because quite substantial proportions – a quarter in the Birmingham survey, for example (AFFOR 1981) – share houses with others, but not with close relatives. The older men may be living with co-tenants and compatriots who originated from the same village, region or caste group, and the women may be living as widows with their deceased husbands' families, but such relationships can be less than fully supportive, occasionally cool and even hostile.

The second note of caution concerns those who *are* living with close relatives but whose experience of isolation and neglect match those of older people on their own. It is quite possible to be isolated in a large family group, to be treated in an offhand or condescending way, to be denied freedom of movement and basic rights to one's own money or goods. Such cases do occur and, when occasional physical abuse comes to light, have been reported to social services departments. In addition to this minority of extreme cases of abuse or neglect there is wider evidence, especially among women, of a number who feel trapped and powerless in their family groups.

Gender and old age

For older Asian people – particularly the women – it is a mixed blessing to be a member of an 'immigrant' minority which maintains traditional expectations and which lives with one foot firmly planted in the old country.

The culture and social institutions which surround them offer security and a sense of identity. For example, it is noted in more than one study of Asian communities that older women may assume a considerable amount of authority and prestige. The most mentioned example is the control of the mother-in-law over daughters-in-law, but Werbner also comments on the ability of older British Asian women to become economically independent and to amend or even override men's decisions. In addition, women play key roles in arranging for suitable marriage partners (with all the significance attached to alliances between kin groups) and in preparing the marriage ceremonies themselves (Bhachu 1985; Werbner 1989). In the Leamington study a significant proportion held a valued status and a set of roles which contributed to relative stability and contentment. They felt they had gained materially and in terms of security when compared with conditions in their native Punjab or in East Africa.

Dhanjal (1976) discusses both the active, positive aspects of life in Britain for Sikh women and the problems they face. She remarks on the way that elements of the Sikh tradition have encouraged respect, if not full equality, for women and have demonstrated their public involvement in social and religious life: for example, women may lead the prayers in the *gurdwara*, or read from the Guru Granth Sahib (Holy Book). And though often having to take unskilled jobs which are demeaning in view of beliefs about caste position (for example, working as cleaners), many Sikh women have at least had the opportunity to earn their own money and to forge friendships with people outside the immediate family. There are also elements of Sikhism which stress that any work is dignified – the important thing is to serve, and to accept those outside one's own religious framework.

Sikh women making chapattis at Smethwick Gurdwara for the Langa *[communal meal]*
Photograph: John Reardon

In a perceptive comment, Dhanjal suggests a growing proportion of older Sikh women at work will begin to resent the remittance of money to their husbands' relatives, especially if an eventual return to India seems less and less likely – this is perhaps a sign of a 'traditional' degree of independence among Sikh women beginning to assert itself in a new direction.

Similarly, though the East African Asian communities are rather a special case, Bhachu's (1985: 72) observations on the role of East African Sikh women illustrate well some of the opportunities provided by 'traditional' roles:

> Older daughters . . . often provide transport for the vast number of things women do on their own in the company of other women. For example, at the time of a marriage, most of the pre-wedding ceremonies were almost entirely 'women-orientated'. A few men would be around the house but did not participate . . .
>
> In sum, East African Sikh women have a considerable amount of freedom and spend a lot of their time on women's activities . . .

Unfortunately, however, there is another side to the role of many women in the Asian communities, the older women included. Resources to support the kinds of activity described by Bhachu may not be available – for example, daughters with cars at their disposal, or access to money which the women themselves are able to draw upon or spend. But even if resources were not the problem, traditional expectations may severely restrict some Asian women's freedom. There are beliefs about modesty and avoiding too much contact with non-relatives; or other concerns about caste which restrict social mixing.

Traditional sanctions and religious prohibitions, including those relating to female seclusion among Muslim communities, have only been partly modified – in some cases actually strengthened – by the transition to life in Britain (Wilson 1978).

Saifullah Khan (1976) argues that rules concerning female seclusion have been imposed in Britain in ways which deny some of the freedoms enjoyed in the old country to move around in the home village or to get involved in trade based in the home. She notes that, in a rural setting in the old country, purdah rules can be relaxed. The intimacy and bonds of village life reduce the need for total seclusion, so that while women are expected to behave modestly, there may be freedom to come and go, to talk with friends beside the village well, or to take food to relatives working in the fields. And as Jeffery (1976) observes, the ability of a family in Pakistan to observe purdah rules depends on economic circumstances: strict purdah entails a strict division of labour, but it may be necessary for the women of poorer families to work outside the home. Consequently, 'there are many variations in the ways in which purdah is observed' (1976: 29).

Purdah rules will have played an important part in the lives of most Pakistani women, unless they are very Westernized (Saifullah Khan 1976), and also will have affected the lives of those in other communities, such as Muslim women from East African countries, or Gujarati women who are Muslim. It is these older women, then, who in the main have come from backgrounds in their countries of origin which, though restrictive, usually enmeshed them in a wide circle of daily contact with others. By contrast, life in Britain has been much narrowed for most of them: unlike most of the older men who have worked in Britain, relatively few older women have had the opportunity to learn any English or to broaden their circle of acquaintances and friends beyond the family.

It could be argued that for older men, too, membership of communities which are 'home' oriented – that is, towards the old country – and which are culturally conservative has led to a certain restrictiveness in their social lives. Just as the older women's status may be partly dependent on whether they have provided children – especially male heirs – for the families they have been married into, so is the older man's status to an extent conditional upon his success in having provided for the household in which he lives; added to this are the responsibilities towards an extended kinship group in Britain and the old country, and perhaps to supporting a public or religious cause. A family's judgement upon a childless woman may be of a harsher nature than upon a man who has fallen short of family expectations to enhance the fortunes of the family group. But Werbner (1989: 130) brings out well the dilemmas faced by Pakistani men who have to balance the competing demands of maintaining a family, a house and in some cases a business in Britain with those of relatives and commercial or community concerns in the old country:

> By contrast to women, migrant men must necessarily examine their status in the wider context of the receiving society. Moreover, in their jobs . . . they are exposed to discrimination . . . Hence they derive their self-esteem in large measure from their position among fellow Pakistanis. Even within

the Pakistani community, however, class status is defined by objective criteria – education, wealth, pedigree and Islamic scholarship.

Similar conclusions could be reached about other South Asian communities, though class position and economic prospects vary. Traditional caste differences among other communities – for example, Hindu communities and, to a lesser extent, the Sikhs – add to the status inequalities among Pakistanis and other Muslims, as described by Werbner.

As among older women, then, the older Asian men's status will in some cases be perceived favourably, dependent on their achievements, loyalty to the community and traditional status. But in other cases the ethnic community, though still acting as a support system in some respects, will not fail to remind the older Asian man of the lower position he must occupy in the hierarchy, in old age as well as in youth. And as with older Afro-Caribbean men, some Asian men experience a sense of disappointment and lack of achievement in not being able to realize the dream of a return to the old country.

Therefore the advantages that older Asian men appear to have over Asian women may not be as clear-cut as first thought. Asian men as a whole have traditionally enjoyed more freedom than women to make friends, escape the drudgery of household chores and spend money on themselves. Yet these patterns of behaviour seem much more common among younger Asian people than among the older men. The first-generation migrant worker has typically worked long hours and, especially in the Midlands and the North, in demanding or hazardous conditions. Equally, the self-employed businessmen and shopkeepers have tended to live completely work-orientated lives, deliberately narrowing their horizons in order to concentrate upon saving, or remitting money home, or meeting family obligations and needs in Britain.

The costs of this way of life may show themselves not only in threats to physical health, but also in alienation from the fuller satisfactions of leisure, education or other mind-broadening experiences. O'Connor's (1972: 124–5) observations on the life experience of Irishmen in Britain – members of another 'immigrant' minority – are applicable to many older Asian men:

> Take, as an example . . . a young man from . . . rural Ireland, who left school at thirteen . . . becomes . . . a partner in a small . . . firm at twenty-five, and a wealthy man in his forties . . . That man may never have had the motivation to read one book . . . [The demands of] success leave many bereft of fulfilment in the 'cultural' areas of their personality.

This sketch of migrant life is of course not always applicable, or may be only partially true of given individuals. But as with other images, such a sketch may help us to understand individual Asians' life histories.

To sum up, we have identified three key characteristics of the social context in which older Asian people live: the 'immigrant minority' quality of their communities, with their ties to the old country; the resilient but changing structure of Asian families; and the strong significance of gender in defining roles for older women and older men in Asian cultures. In the following discussion of individuals' experiences, these three key characteristics should be borne in mind.

Personal accounts of growing old

The range of examples which follow illustrates the diversity of experience of individual Asian men and women. We begin with those who were relatively content and end with those who saw themselves as disadvantaged in many ways.

There are some examples of individual experience which illustrate social engagement and a degree of success in ageing. Mr A, for example, was a Sikh aged 72 living in Handsworth, Birmingham. Though living alone, he saw his nearby daughter and her children regularly; his own wife had died before she could join him in Britain, and Mr A had no family in India. He proudly discussed his daily task of escorting a score or more children from his own street to school, then meeting them in the afternoon to bring them back safely. Mr A thoroughly enjoyed this role: it gave him contact not only with the children, but also with their parents and with other relatives as well as with passers-by and the school; this 'job', though unpaid, also provided a sense of worth.

Mr A is unusual in taking on this kind of voluntary activity, but less unusual in demonstrating traits of self-reliance and successful ageing among older Asian men living alone.

> When I came to Britain, I thought I would save lots of money, live like 'Sadar' (a prince, lord) and have everything done by servants. I have not been able to do this, I have to do everything myself. But I have never feared old age.

Mr A went on to describe how he had recently enjoyed a birthday party of one of his grandchildren. Despite a hard working life in India and in a foundry in the West Midlands, and the loss of his wife, Mr A expressed satisfaction with most of the circumstances in which he lived, and especially with his accommodation in a ground-floor council flat; in all, the proximity of close relatives and his outlook on life result in Mr A fitting a category of 'socially engaged, successful ageing' quite closely.

The same might also be said of Mr E, another Sikh who was aged 68 but who had migrated to Britain at a relatively 'old' age (52). As with Mr A, Mr E had also worked on the land in the Punjab, and had migrated to a foundry job in Wolverhampton. At the time of the survey he was living with his wife only, but had moved to Birmingham on retirement in order to be nearer to relatives and friends. Mr E summarized his position as follows:

> I think I am much better off in Britain now than I would be if old in India, in all respects – money for food, clothes, other things. I have no worries. We don't need any help for anything, my wife and myself do everything.

Again, we have an example of someone who, though living in an 'immigrant' minority, had no strong wish to go 'home' and apparently did not suffer at all from a sense of loss or yearning for the old country; on the contrary, Mr E had adjusted happily to an old age in Britain and mentioned frequent contact with a brother who lived nearby and many other relatives and friends.

A few of the women interviewed in the Birmingham 'follow-up' survey (Blakemore 1984) also illustrate aspects of successful ageing. Mrs K, a 64-year-old Gujarati woman who had migrated seven years previously to Birmingham from India, spoke in a positive and uninhibited way about her new life in Britain. Mrs K lived in a large household with two of her sons, their wives and children; a third son and his family lived nearby.

> All my children were all here, so no matter what, you have to like it and try to adjust to the way of life here. The area was populated with white people. The people were and still are very nice, and helpful, I've never had any trouble from anyone. Now this area is more populated with Asian people . . . Comparing myself to old people in India I am much better off, because if you are poor in India you can't afford a doctor. Only thing is, the social life in India is much better, the weather here mainly stops you going out a lot.

Mrs K described her full active social life in greater depth: her daily round of shopping, housework, visiting shops and the local temple, as well as day trips in the summer and Sundays spent visiting friends. This is a clear example of a female making a successful transition from late middle age to early 'old age'. Mrs K was finding fulfilment not only in sharing housework and child-rearing, but also in influencing the family life of her two sons and their wives. Mrs K's husband had died and she saw herself as being the representative of the original Indian-born element of the family. She illustrates the possibility that widows in the South Asian families may gain power and family responsibility as well as lose it.

Others, however, are beginning to experience old age as a period of disengagement and some loss of status and well-being. Stoic acceptance and low expectations among them may disguise the position of such women. It is possible that psychological disengagement underlies this acceptance and apparent passivity, and there is speculation that either Hindu or Hindu-influenced beliefs play a part in fostering such attitudes among men as well as women (Vatuk 1980): according to Hindu philosophy, old age should be a time for disengaging from social relationships and material considerations, and for developing one's inner spiritual life in preparation for the next phase of existence. If this is so, one would expect Hindus in Gujarati and other Indian communities to be most affected, as well as Sikhs, whose beliefs are close to those of Hinduism in many respects.

Our case-study evidence does not lend much support to these speculations, though it should be remembered that the interviews were not conducted with hypotheses about religious belief and attitudes to old age in mind. Future research, focused on possible links between religious belief, culture and life in old age in the minority communities, could throw up interesting findings. What does emerge from our individual accounts is a strong connection between older Asians' *social* circumstances or the networks available to them and their degree of involvement or engagement. It was not readily apparent that inner or psychological drives are the primary cause of disengagement.

Mrs C, for example, was a Sikh widow of 71 who lived with her daughter. As her daughter was no longer married and no children lived with them, Mrs C's family network was much more circumscribed than most respondents'. It emerged in interview that Mrs C had been 'brought up by the community' in India: orphaned and impoverished, she had had no immediate family to look after her. Yet Mrs C was uncomplaining, active, talkative and alert, if socially disengaged. She had learned to be self-sufficient from an early age.

Mrs C's experience is analagous to that of the older Asian men Barker (1984) described as 'pioneer' migrants, even though Mrs C had lived in Britain for only 17 years. As with older male 'pioneer' migrants, she lived from day to day in a rather frugal and detached way, not expecting much company and not regretting the loss of former ties with her in-laws. If and when such people become frail and dependent on either 'community' or institutional care, their personal histories of self-reliance will mean that they have a particularly sharp need for recognition of their independence: they are not used to 'being helped' so that, in addition to coping with all the other changes associated with loss of physical mobility or illness, they may have a difficult time trying to understand and deal with the unfamiliar expectations of care-givers or social service workers.

Other case studies show a number of older Asians, especially women, who are apparently fully integrated in larger households but who reveal a loss or lack of significant and deep relationships. Mrs P, for example, was a woman in her late fifties who had come to Britain from Kenya in 1968. Though living with her four sons, their wives and six grandchildren, Mrs P was close to only one daughter-in-law, whom she described as 'the one who looks after me and does all the work'. Mrs P had been widowed eight years previously. She described the shoemaking business her late father and her husband had been working in, and her own work in Kenya as a seamstress. All these things had taken place 'in a different world'. Mrs P had not been out to visit anyone at all for a whole month before the interview (which took place during a summer), but despite this did not seem to be particularly lonely or depressed. She confessed that, though she had not liked Britain at all when she had arrived, she was getting used to the country. She filled her days with domestic routine and felt that she was better off in Britain than in either Kenya or India.

Similarly, Mr D, a much older person (82), had come from East Africa and, like Mrs P, lived in a large household (eleven people, including two sons and their families). Though a Muslim, he was not particularly interested in religion or the social activities associated with the mosque. He saw old age as a time for 'just resting and relaxing at home'; he had looked foward to being looked after by his sons and their families, 'as I did for my parents'. Though the potential for social engagement was high, however, Mr D did not enjoy particularly close relationships with his family or with others: in his case the change from East Africa had distanced him somewhat from his immediate social environment rather than acting as a cementing tie with other 'East African' family members; there was also some evidence of psychological withdrawal or disengagement, showing that – though having a close family and other relationships is of prime importance – the significance of inner change should not be discounted.

The above cases stand for a considerable number of older Asian people who are basically uncomplaining and as yet have made little demand upon social services, but whose position is potentially problematic in the sense that they are either actually socially isolated to to some degree socially or emotionally adrift from the family groups they are living with. At the same time they have little sense of belonging to the wider urban society which surrounds them, and many have worries about being excluded or demeaned by white people. The following examples underline these themes but also illustrate how problems become sharper and needs greater in some older Asian people's lives.

Mrs N, a Sikh woman of 74, spoke for many other older Asian women in these circumstances. Mrs N lived with a son, daughter-in-law and grand-children. She was a widow and her oldest son had also died, in India. On the face of it, Mrs N was well integrated with her family, regularly met with relatives in nearby Wolverhampton and visited the neighbourhood *gurdwara* often. But a longer interview revealed that, though she rarely complained to members of her immediate family, she frequently experienced depression and loneliness. At the same time, she recognized that her grandchildren were very supportive and felt guilty about expressing her inner feelings.

Above all, Mrs N's problems stemmed from unhappiness about what she saw as an irrevocable split between the family in India and in Britain. She felt closer to India than to life in Birmingham, though there was a tremendous pull to stay with her British grandchildren. Not only was she still experiencing grief over the death of her husband, 17 years before, and of her son; she also talked of how her image of her own old age – which she had anticipated as one of relaxation and being looked after – had been shattered. She frequently experienced backache and stomach pains, symptoms which she felt were expressions of her mental state (for further discussion of connections between migration and mental health, see Chapter 7).

It also emerged in the interview that Mrs N had been very worried about the reception she had received from the immigration authorities on her last entry into Britain. Though entitled to stay, she had felt intimidated and frightened. And three months before the interview, her third son – who had been visiting the family in Britain and whose presence 'was the highlight of my stay in England' – had left hurriedly for India because he was no longer permitted to stay by the immigration authorities.

While Mrs N's case illustrates divided loyalties, Mr I exemplified isolation. Mr I, a 70-year-old Sikh, had migrated to Britain in 1965 and had found factory work in Smethwick, then in Birmingham. He lived with a son, but the latter had no wife or children with him and had relatively little to do with Mr I. Mr I himself had been widowed, and though he had a number of sons and daughters in the United Kingdom he did not see much of them. However, Mr I was uncomplaining and observed with some resignation that 'in India we all lived together'. It gradually emerged that Mr I was very lonely and, though he had accepted his problem and felt there was little he could do about it, he added at the end of the interview: 'I want to be looked after by a big happy family, but my son and daughter-in-law don't want me to live with them'.

In other aspects of life Mr I seemed to define his circumstances as non-problematic (he was reasonably well, and he thought the medical services were much better in Britain than in India), but then shifted to another tack, adding 'they look down on you because you can't speak English' and 'I think they want to get rid of us'. In terms of economic well-being and the basic provision of health services, Mr I felt grateful for being able to live in Britain, but this apparent contentment was shot through with fears of racial discrimination and hostility from the service providers.

Finally, there is the category of individual cases which might best be described as those who felt they were ageing unsuccessfully, in their own terms, and who articulated their feelings about this. One example of this was Mr J, a dissatisfied ex-teacher, though we should be clear that it was not just the well educated who expressed dissatisfaction with their circumstances.

Mr J had come to Britain from Malawi, where he had been a teacher for many years. Aged 68, he had migrated after his retirement at 62 to join his son and family in Birmingham. As Mr J's father had been a teacher and Mr J a teacher himself all his working life, it is not surprising that he judged the circumstances around him with a rather critical eye. He thought the British environment was 'very dull, with bad houses and bad streets – a dirty place altogether.' As for Malawi:

> They don't want us because the Africans are taking over. I don't think they want us in this country as well . . . that's why we live in bad areas like this with bad houses. We are scared to go out alone in the evenings.

It was not clear whether Mr J was expressing disappointment which resulted from a gap between idealized expectations of life in Britain and reality, or whether his dissatisfactions stemmed from simply having ended up in a set of circumstances he had never wanted. Either way, he clearly missed many aspects of his former life in Malawi – social contacts, servants, good health services and the warm climate. As he stated: 'I had looked forward to my old age . . . in a large house in Malawi, and not worrying about anything.'

Mr J clearly illustrates the significance of subjective perceptions of the ageing experience. Objectively, Mr J was well off: he enjoyed good health and was well supported by his wife, son, daughter-in-law and many other relatives and friends in Britain; he continued to read widely, enjoyed gardening and visiting other people. But he was not happy, and said so.

On the other hand, there are significant numbers of older Asian people who are unhappy and who have problems by anyone's standard. Mrs S, for example, was aged 63 and crippled by chronic arthritis. She found the disease both painful and very restricting. She saw her problem as a general predicament of growing old in Britain:

> It is too cold here. I never thought it (old age) would be like this. My health is worse and we have no social life. I have never liked it here and didn't want to come. There is too much racial hatred and we are not wanted.

Not only did Mrs S seem to have few ties with relatives or others in the local Sikh community, but also her husband's previous employment in the armed forces in Malaysia had the effect of cutting her off from her roots in India; she had lost touch with her parents when younger, for example, and did not know when or how they had died. The 'marooned' image (see Chapter 5) best described her unhappy situation.

This also applied to Mrs B, a Sikh woman in her late sixties who lived alone. Mrs B's account of her earlier life in Birmingham showed that she had been quite happy. In recent years, however, she had been widowed and her children had married and moved away; she had no close ties with any relatives now, either in Britain or in India. As she put it: 'People are too busy making money nowadays. Nobody cares, but it is the same in India.' Mrs B's health was deteriorating and, among other things, her eyesight was failing; however, an operation to remove cataracts was about to take place.

In contrast to Mrs S, however, Mrs B did have a lifeline of support in the form of good neighbours. In fact she was heavily dependent on them not only for social contact but also because they helped her with housework, cooking and maintaining her property. However supportive, though, neighbourly contact could hardly make up for an old age which Mrs B saw clearly as disappointing. She articulated her sadness, saying:

> I was not prepared for old age. I never thought about it. If I had known it would be like this, I would have ended it all a long time ago.

Conclusion

The aims of this chapter have been to show how certain common themes affect older Asian people and are revealed in their own accounts of their lives. First, there is a certain ambivalence about ageing in Britain, with a mixture of negative and positive feelings even among those who appear to be most committed to growing older in a 'foreign' land.

Second, there has been continuity of ethnic identity even among East African Asians, with the majority still attached to cultural traditions (though these are changing and adapting) and – except for East African communities – living in relatively large family groups. However, it is important not to assume that Asian family structures and norms will continue to adapt and change in a step-by-step way. While myths of a complete breakdown of the Asian family can be disregarded, there is a real possibility of fundamental change in some aspects of family life and inter-generational relationships in at least some of the Asian communities.

At the moment the relative rarity of older people living alone is noticeable, especially when compared with the white majority or with older Afro-Caribbean people. But this should be placed alongside possibilities of loneliness and marginalization felt by individuals living in family groups, or with people from the same background. And older Asians' perception of their position as being different from expectations can lead to varying degrees of disillusion.

Finally, whether Asian men or women fare well in old age has been shown to depend partly on their individual outlook and strength of personality (as in the case of Mr A), though the strong influence of a gender 'division of labour' severely constrains older Asian people from finding their own solutions. This may be relevant, for example, in the case of an older man trying to learn housekeeping skills, or an older woman coming to terms with money management or trying to make and keep friendships outside the home.

7

Health, illness and health services

In this chapter we will examine the health needs of older black and Asian people. This will entail a consideration of a range of factors. To begin with, it will be important to set their health needs in the context of debates about race and health generally. The question of 'double jeopardy' in health has already been touched upon, but in this chapter the debate on health needs will be extended.

Above all, it seems important not to treat older black people as exotic specimens of ageing among whom there are completely distinctive patterns of health and disease. This is not to deny that there are some special needs or problems among a proportion of older black people. Nor should the influence of cultural or ethnic factors on health or utilization of medical services be disregarded – they have important effects among all ethnic groups (see, for example, Zola 1966; Holzberg 1982). The point is that such ethnically distinctive features should not be allowed to overshadow the discussion.

The health of older black people is the product of a variety of individual actions and social forces, not least the impact of racism and racial disadvantage in health service provision but including other things such as environmental and occupational factors. How much weight should be given to each of these major influences is, of course, an open question; the discussion in this chapter will emphasize the contested nature of the debate, though some broad conclusions will be drawn at the end.

Race, health and medical services

Johnson (1984: 228) refers to a 'substantial and growing literature' on minority groups and health. While such a literature is developing, it is not always of immediate relevance to those interested in the health of older black and Asian people. Much of it is addressed to questions of health concerning children or younger adults (see, for example, Karseras and Hopkins 1987) or to general problems of race relations and inequality in the health service (Mares *et al.* 1985) but not specifically how these problems apply to older people.

And despite the growing interest mentioned by Johnson, discussion of race and health still does not occupy a central place in debates on policy, at least in Britain. In comparison with the amount of attention given to health inequalities between social classes or between the North and South of the United Kingdom, race and ethnicity are hardly mentioned. For example, in Townsend and Davidson's (1982: 58–60) first summary of the Black report there are but two pages on race, ethnicity and health. Standard texts on race relations (see, for example, Pilkington 1984; Stone 1985; Cashmore and Troyna 1989) also neglect the relationship between race and health in favour of well-trodden areas such as education, employment and housing.

Perhaps these omissions are at least partly accounted for by lack of evidence. It may be recalled, from our earlier discussion of mortality rates among Asian and Afro-Caribbean people (see Chapter 4), that hypotheses about double jeopardy have been difficult to test because until recently 'race has rarely been assessed in official censuses and surveys' (Townsend *et al.* 1988: 50); commentators wishing to draw links between race and health have had to rely on indirect indicators such as place of birth or nationality.

One review of the literature concluded that 'there is no systematic or detailed evidence available about the health of black people in Britain' (Runnymede Trust 1980: 109). Later, McNaught (1984: 15) referred to 'the virtual absence of ethnically sensitive health statistics in the United Kingdom', arguing that this seriously hinders the development of effective strategies to meet minority needs. Admittedly, the inclusion of questions in the 1991 population census on race and 'ethnic' identity, and on the occurrence of 'long-standing illness' will improve matters, though the questions themselves are generalized and will not facilitate much in-depth analysis of patterns of health and illness.

Although apparent unconcern in central government is probably the major reason for the lack of a national overview of racial differences in health and illness, a contributory factor might be a worry about the danger of a racist backlash. The Runnymede Trust (1980: 108), for example, mentions an 'over-utilization' scare of the 1960s, when discontent was stirred by selective reference to statistics on the use of maternity services by immigrant women. The scare distracted attention from an actual under-utilization of health services by black people. More recently, the introduction of health service charges to overseas visiting patients has led to allegations that some hospitals began to demand passport identification from black patients, irrespective of their nationality. Understandably, in such an atmosphere of mistrust, some leaders of minority ethnic communites are wary of official attempts to collect information on health service use. So while evidence is accumulating, either from local community health or social surveys, it is the lack of a full national picture that is startling.

Apart from these difficulties, there are even more fundamental problems in using the term 'race' as an explanation for differences in health. While differences in rates of disease between racial groups might be observed, this does not mean that either 'race' itself (in the physical or biological sense) or racism and racial disadvantage are necessarily causing these differences. Racial categories may be variables which summarize other causal factors. As Antonovsky and Bernstein (1977: 459) say of class, 'social class itself does not cause infant mortality – it is a powerful "zeroing in" variable'. Sometimes race or ethnicity may operate this way, such as when an observed difference in a disease rate may mask other causal factors – the incidence of smoking in different ethnic groups, for example. Or what may appear to be a racial difference in health between two groups might disappear when another variable such as social class or gender, is controlled for.

One of the main advantages of looking at the relationship between ageing and race is that we may begin to understand how persistent racial and ethnic differences are, or how far they are eroded by age. However, it must also be remembered that in some instances race and racism *are* of primary significance as causal factors.

As McNaught (1984: 26) notes, it is difficult to ascertain just how much racial discrimination there is in the National Health Service. He suggests that the *perceptions* people in minority ethnic groups have of medical services are as important as the actual extent of racism in service delivery. The discussion which follows will examine what appear to be main sources of disquiet or worry about health services among black elderly people, in so far as these have been touched on by various research studies. We will also examine patterns of use of medical services by older black people and try to indicate what these tell us about the quality of health services received and what factors, for example, may impede good communication between them and medical practitioners.

Health in old age

Before focusing on health services, however, it seems important to look at what we know about the health status of ageing black people. Are the health needs and problems faced by this predominantly 'young elderly' group beginning to correspond to the 'diseases of old age' experienced by the majority, for example? Or are there distinctive ethnic patterns of health and illness of continuing importance to older black people?

On the question of differences being accounted for by racial inequality, some commentators do seem to see these as having a primary significance. Norman (1985: 61) for example, suggests that

> poor housing conditions . . . give rise to health hazards from overcrowding and inadequate sanitation and heating. Men who cannot stay in their homes or lodgings during the day may be forced to wander in parks and shopping centres in all weathers and may try to blot out present reality and past trauma with alcohol. Women who are afraid to go out or unaccustomed to doing so may get too little exercise and sunshine as well as becoming socially isolated and depressed. Inadequate income may result in poor diet and insufficient warm clothing. A lifetime of work in dangerous and unhealthy conditions – on building sites, steamy kitchens, in rag-trade sweatshops and in the least protected and hardest labouring

jobs in industry – can create chronic illness and disability. In addition, for the present immigrant generation, there is the stress arising from facing old age 'in a strange land', homesickness for the country of origin, and for those who are 'black', the constant tension of living with racial harassment and discrimination.

Though this statement summarizes powerfully the kinds of disadvantage some black people may face, it can lead to an unquestioning assumption that all are equally disadvantaged in health when this may not be so (see Chapter 4). The aim of the discussion which follows is partly to disentangle the conflicting evidence we have about health among the various minority groups, because we may find that key sub-divisions make all the difference – for example, between men and women, 'young' old and 'old' old, between ethnic groups and between urban communities.

Broad assumptions that there are sharp racial inequalities in the use of health services also ignore the contested nature of the evidence. One community survey (Donaldson 1986) of older Asian people in Leicester reported that the minority population seemed to differ little from the majority in the extent of illnesses suffered. And in terms of being able to perform basic activities of daily living unaided, it was concluded that 'the Asian elderly were similar to their indigenous counterparts' (1986: 1081). Another piece of medical research, by Ebrahim *et al.* (1987), shows that there are some significant health problems affecting older black people, but suggests that there is 'no evidence to support the contention that elderly immigrants are under-using hospital resources' (1987: 254).

The latter survey was designed to find out whether older Afro-Caribbean and Asian people are less likely than indigenous white elderly people to be admitted to hospital. As mentioned above, data on use of medical services may be interpreted in different ways. An obvious limitation, which the authors point out, is that a study of hospital discharges will not take into account a whole range of illnesses which may not merit hospital treatment but which are of great significance to older people – for example, depression and other mental conditions as well as cognitive decline, urinary incontinence, or deafness. But even within the category of hospital illnesses, there are some problems in interpreting the meanings of findings on rates of hospitalization. A *lower* or *equal* rate of hospitalization among older black people, compared with older whites, may mean that health services are failing to pick up the true extent of illness. Thus a lower rate of hospitalization reflects a degree of racial insensitivity and a neglect of minority needs, not rates of illness. It may, alternatively, mean that health among older black people is at least as good, perhaps somewhat better in certain respects, than health among older whites.

Though these are competing explanations, they could in reality work together as factors to explain rates of hospitalization; for example, *some* of a relatively low rate of hospitalization among older black people could be explained by neglect or racism, but some could be explained also by objectively lower rates of certain diseases.

Turning to explanations for *higher* rates of hospitalization, we may be faced with the following possibilities:

1 A higher incidence of disease among minority elderly people, but no greater problems in respect of access to hospital treatment. Higher than average rates of hospitalization therefore reflect disease rates reasonably accurately.

2 A higher incidence of disease among minority elderly people which is not *fully* reflected in hospitalization rates. Although hospitalization rates may be higher than among the majority, the extent of illness among the minority may be greater yet, suggesting a considerable amount of unmet need or problems of referral and access to hospital.

3 A lower or equal incidence of disease among the minority, but a higher than average tendency for minority elderly patients either to be referred to hospital or to seek hospital treatment.

In order to examine the relative importance of all these possibilities, research of an ambitious kind would have to be carried out. Nevertheless, Ebrahim *et al.*'s (1987) study does identify certain interesting patterns in the types of complaint patients had been treated for. And by comparing these findings on hospital discharge with other community-based surveys, we are able to make some judgements about both the extent of illness and the use of medical services among older minority people.

First, Ebrahim *et al.*'s hospital survey confirms other major findings on ethnic differences in common diseases among younger black and white people (see Chapter 4). Afro-Caribbeans over pensionable age are exposed to a *higher* risk of stroke, when compared with discharge rates among whites born in Britain, but there is a *lower* risk of heart attack among the older Afro-Caribbeans. Older Asian people are at greater risk of experiencing heart attack than stroke, when compared to patients born in Britain (Ebrahim *et al.* 1987: 251). As the authors note, these findings correspond quite closely with those of Cruickshank *et al.* (1980) and others. For Afro-Caribbeans, the findings represent about twice the risk of mortality from stroke but about half the risk of death from myocardial infarction compared with the general population.

The Nottingham study by Ebrahim *et al.* also identified a number of other health problems. These were, for Asian patients, higher than expected rates of diabetes, gastrointestinal bleeding and asthma. The authors speculate about the impact of dietary change and migratory adjustment, or 'a rapidly altered way of life', on the first two complaints. As other studies (for example, Cruickshank *et al.* 1980) have also mentioned higher than average rates of diabetes in Afro-Caribbean as well as Asian communities, there are grounds for investigating further some possible links between migration, diet and diabetes among older black and Asian people.

Three other significant health problems are mentioned: first, femur fractures are a relatively serious problem among older Asians, but not Afro-Caribbeans, highlighting debates about osteomalacia ('brittle bone' disease) and supposed Vitamin D deficiency; second, an above-average risk among older Asians of contacting or developing tuberculosis (a problem which calls for sensitive handling by primary health care and hospital services), and third, relatively high rates among both Asian and Afro-Caribbean patients of treatment for cataract. This latter problem does not seem to have been much discussed before in terms of the needs of older minority people, though the authors refer to other work which indicates higher morbidity among those originating from tropical countries, as a result of exposure to strong sunlight and to risks of dehydration.

Interestingly, the community surveys by Bhalla and Blakemore (1981), which contains evidence on self-reported illness, also revealed a relatively high proportion of Afro-Caribbeans (61 per cent) and of older Asians (53 per cent) with some sort of sight problem. By no means all of this may be attributed to cataract, though cataract may be an important contributory factor. The percentage of older white people reporting sight difficulties was almost as high (52 per cent), but the white sample in the Birmingham survey was comprised of a significantly older group and we would expect to find, among the younger Asians and Afro-Caribbeans, appreciably fewer sight problems. As sight problems are common, even in a relatively young population of ageing Asian and Afro-Caribbean people, this has implications for leisure, social and domiciliary services as well as for the provision of adequate medical and ophthalmic services.

The problems of osteomalacia and tuberculosis illustrate the dangers of seeking one major explanation for apparently 'ethnic' or 'racial' differences in disease. The history of rickets and osteomalacia in Britain shows that lack of exposure to sunlight (as a result of atmospheric pollution, lack of outdoor amenities, a home-centred lifestyle, and so on) increases its incidence because the body's own production of Vitamin D in sunlight is the major source. However, a lack of Vitamin D in the diet will often tip the balance towards clinically observed disease, even though less than 10 per cent of the Vitamin D we require is gained this way. There is a lack of Vitamin D in most British diets, including those of the majority (Mares *et al.* 1985). The addition of Vitamin D to margarine and other foods has significantly reduced the incidence of rickets and osteomalacia. But, as many have noted (for example, Donovan 1984), the policy of adding Vitamin D to staple foods has not been extended to the commonest foods used by Asian communities, such as chapatti flour.

Tuberculosis also shows the multicausal origins of differences in disease rates. Undue emphasis was initially laid on higher prevalence of tuberculosis in migrants' former homelands as the explanation for higher rates among immigrants in Britain. However, a careful consideration of the evidence shows that many sufferers acquired tuberculosis in Britain, and that the incidence of the disease was at a low rate in some migrants' countries – for example, in some Caribbean states (Donovan 1984: 665). As Donovan (1984: 665) concludes:

> most published papers eventually reach the same conclusion: that it is the environment of the inner cities and the disadvantages experienced by the black population that have helped to maintain tuberculosis among them, and that only if and when these conditions are improved . . . will tuberculosis be controlled and reduced.

Among other health problems investigated in the Birmingham (AFFOR 1981) survey, dental problems among Asians and Afro-Caribbeans and walking/foot problems among Afro-Caribbeans also seemed to be as common as they were among a retired white sample of higher average age. Some caution must be exercised here, mainly because we are in the field of cross-cultural comparison of the perceived severity or significance of illness. If anything, however, these perceptions may underestimate incidence, especially among older Asian people. The Birmingham (AFFOR) survey showed that:

> in relation to the elderly respondents' view of their lives and the improvements they seek, health-related problems were mentioned by 15 per cent of the Afro-Caribbean, 13 per cent of the Asian and 25 per cent of the European elderly . . . The minority elderly, in particular those of Asian origin, have rather modest expectations of life and the level of health to be expected in old age. Over half of the Asian group could think of nothing to improve life beyond present levels of satisfaction.
> (Blakemore 1982: 72)

Of the four kinds of health problem identified in the Birmingham survey (sight, mobility/walking, dental and hearing) only the latter was reported by the older white sample with greater frequency (Blakemore 1982: 71), though even in this respect over a fifth of the Asian elders said they had hearing difficulties compared with 7 per cent of the Afro-Caribbeans and over 30 per cent of the whites.

The Birmingham evidence, combined with the more recent hospital survey by Ebrahim *et al.*, tends to suggest that, either in terms of common illnesses such as cardio-vascular disease or in terms of 'ageing problems', the health of older black people is not as good as might be expected. As Ebrahim *et al.* show, their rates of hospitalization for a number of diagnoses are higher than among their white counterparts, while in Birmingham we find their health – in self-reported terms – is no better than that among older white pensioners.

Given these findings, Donaldson's (1986) conclusions about the health of elderly Asian people in Leicester are somewhat surprising. Donaldson's study, a survey of 726 people derived from general practice lists, reported on physical functioning; it also included information on diet, incidence of cigarette smoking and on urinary incontinence. In these respects, the health of the Asian respondents appeared to be little different from a comparable group of older white people. For example, Donaldson notes that about a fifth of the Asian elders experienced urinary incontinence occasionally or frequently, and that over half of the over-75s are not fully independent in their daily activities – but these proportions are in line with the general population.

However, this survey needs to be put in context. As Donaldson (1986: 1082) himself notes, health needs and patterns of illness vary among the Asian communities in different parts of Britain. It is significant that Donaldson's survey dealt in the main with people who had come to Britain from countries in East Africa. In those countries, almost two-fifths had been in skilled employment and another two-fifths had worked in retail or other businesses. Admittedly, over half had been in unskilled jobs since arriving in Britain, thus experiencing a loss of status and income and, perhaps, less healthy working conditions than before. But it is very likely that the former living standards of the majority of older people in Donaldson's survey, together with their expectations of health and of medical services, will have had a decisive effect on their health since settling in Leicester. Two other aspects of the sample should be noted. The first is that four-fifths have ancestral links with one region of India – Gujarat – and the remainder have families originating mainly in the Punjab. The Leicester survey is by and large one of Gujaratis, and there may be a range of ethnic factors affecting their health which do not affect other ethno-religious Asian communities in quite the same way. The second important aspect of the survey is that it took place in Leicester, a city which has experienced some economic problems, but not nearly as many as those urban districts in the nearby West Midlands, where unemployment and poorer environmental conditions tend to cause ill health. Asian men in the West Midlands, for example, are more likely to have worked in heavy industry, with its risks of injury and occupational disease, than older men in Leicester.

Interestingly, a more recent survey by Ebrahim *et al.* (1991: 59) of the prevalence of illness among Gujaratis in north London found that though 'common chronic diseases affected Asians more frequently than the indigenous population . . . problems of old age (falls, incontinence and depression) affected Asian subjects less often'. Again, these findings hint at complex patterns of health and illness among the various communities. The Gujarati sample were relatively economically advantaged, often enjoying a higher standard of living than local white people, but in this case economic advantage had not reduced risks of heart disease or diabetes. The lower rates of problems associated with ageing are accounted for by the relative youth of this sample.

The above findings contrast with those of Fenton (1986), whose reports on health among Afro-Caribbean and South Asian middle-aged and elderly people in a depressed part of central Bristol paint a much bleaker picture. While Fenton's survey included only a small number of people aged over 60, the respondents' self-assessments of their health suggest that older Afro-Caribbeans experience more illness than either Asian or white pensioners. Fenton (1986: 44) notes: 'Two-thirds of the 60+ year old West Indians reported a health cause for regular medical visits, as against a half in the other groups'. In some respects these differences are observable in the Birmingham survey (Bhalla and Blakemore 1981), which also shows that Afro-Caribbeans are the most likely to say they have major health problems (Blakemore 1982: 71). We also found, in Birmingham, that the Afro-Caribbeans were the most frequently hospitalized group (Blakemore 1982: 70).

However, while over two-fifths of older Afro-Caribbeans had been hospitalized during the previous year, it is the high proportion of Afro-Caribbean *women* – almost half – needing hospital treatment who account for the difference between the Afro-Caribbean community and other ethnic groups. In terms of attention to special needs, whether these are for preventive medicine, health education or social support during and after treatment, it would therefore seem that Afro-Caribbean women should be given a high priority. Fenton's (1986) study highlights the familiar problems of hypertensive disease and diabetes as being particularly problematic for this group; his reportage of older Afro-Caribbeans' accounts of their lives is eloquent testimony to the impact of stressful and unhealthy working conditions on their health in later life.

An older man whose wife is ill, makes preparations to return to Jamaica
Photograph: Abdullah Badwi

However, the apparent differences in the amount of illness among Afro-Caribbean and Asian older people do not justify a hard-and-fast conclusion that most in the former group are always in poorer health than most in the latter. To begin with, as noted above, we are not dealing with two 'communities' or two geographical locations, but a variety of different Afro-Caribbean and Asian communities. As with the differences between older Asian people in Leicester and those in other communities, it is quite likely that average levels of health among some Afro-Caribbean communities are better than they appear to be in Bristol and Birmingham.

Conversely, we found that while the Asians comprised the group with the largest proportion saying they had no serious health problems, they also included the largest proportion with *multiple* health problems (Blakemore 1982: 71) – that is, three of the four 'problems of living' identified in the Birmingham survey (problems with sight, hearing, mobility and dental problems) and/or additional problems identified by respondents, such as heart disease. And, as noted by others who have studied relations between Asian people and the health service (for example, Henley 1979; Rack 1982), there is often an understandable reluctance to divulge intimate information to unknown outsiders. It is very likely that all the surveys using questionnaires as the primary research instrument have underestimated the amount of illness among older Asians, and particularly among women.

The question of women's needs illustrates how misunderstandings may arise if physical mobility or going out of the home are used in an uncritical way to assess health. In Birmingham, we found significant differences not only between men and women in terms of going out, but also between Afro-Caribbean men – who go out less often – and white and Asian men (Blakemore 1982: 72). Older Asian men are the most 'active' in this respect, and interestingly their habit of going out of the home daily has not yet begun to decline with age – as many of the over-70s go out daily as those aged 70 or below. As there are such marked differences between the sexes, and between Asians and Afro-Caribbeans, these patterns of physical functioning and social contact are clearly much more to do with social norms and constraints than with health or illness.

However, physical frailty and health problems are not unimportant in explaining patterns of activity among older Asian and Afro-Caribbean people. As this population ages, such physical complaints will have increasing significance. It is important, though, to view these health problems in a social context. Older Asian men, for example, may struggle against cold weather and physical ailments to go out daily, partly through choice but also, in some cases, because they have been edged out of the house.

Equally, it is important to note that others – Afro-Caribbean women in particular – seem to be experiencing rather heavy burdens of illness which may be preventing them from getting about as much as they would like. The large-scale Coventry (1986) survey also confirmed the Birmingham evidence that about a third of older Asian people experience at least some difficulties in walking outside the home. However, in Birmingham over three-fifths of Afro-Caribbean women were found to have mobility problems (AFFOR 1981). For some explanation, we may consider Fenton's (1986) research, which includes a number of biographical accounts of unhealthy or stressful working lives – for example, jobs which have required a lot of standing or lifting, or which have repeatedly strained limbs and backs. To these problems may be added hypertension and diabetes, both of which have a higher than average incidence among Afro-Caribbean women and which can restrict mobility.

Experience of health services

We have already discussed inequalities in rates of mortality and disease between older black and Asian people, on the one hand, and the majority, on the other (see Chapter 4); inequalities in access to and use of services have also been touched on. To complete the picture we also need to consider black and Asian older people's experiences of health services. Inequalities in the quantitative sense (for example, rates of use of various services) are important, but it is equally important to look at the social or human context in which these unequal patterns exist – the ways in which the health service has responded (or failed to respond) to older people in minority ethnic groups, and how older black patients perceive health services.

As these topics raise questions about the interpersonal or face-to-face aspects of health care, and how practical lessons may be learned in order to improve communication, it may help to know that we have continued discussion of interpersonal or practitioner–user relationships in Chapter 8, under the heading of 'social services', though we hope that much of that material will also be applicable in the health services. However, there are some leading questions on the delivery and experience of health services which we will consider now.

There is disturbing evidence from a number of studies that black and Asian people suffer from various forms of racial discrimination when they use the British National Health Service. Pearson (1986: 102) believes that racism is 'central' in 'structuring black people's health and experience of the health service'. Likewise, Rathwell and Phillips (1986: 262) criticize existing training of NHS personnel, which they think 'does not get at the root of the problem – racial prejudice and hostility from health service personnel which may stem from embarrassment . . . or misconceptions'.

Much of the evidence has been well summarized by Mares *et al.* (1985). There are weaknesses in the research design of some of the studies they refer to – for example, in the use of anecdotal 'horror stories' or failure to compare evidence of mistreatment of white patients with black patients – but it is clear from the sheer weight of evidence that the NHS is experienced by many black patients as racially discriminatory. There are problems of racism at different levels:

- *Direct racism:* for example intolerance, hostility or coolness toward black patients. This may be seen not only in angry or impatient attitudes among staff – an intolerant 'take it or leave it' view – but also in condescending or patronizing attitudes. It might be assumed that the hospital's or white staff's way of doing things is intrinsically superior to the ideas of minority ethnic communities on healing, diet, or treatment of patients.
- *Racism at the organizational level:* within the administrative unit (general practice, hospital, community health centre) there may be a failure to recognize that we live in a multiracial society. No one will have thought about the need for translation services, for example, or to take account of dietary needs/religious prescriptions beyond the well-established ones (such as for vegetarians, or for Jewish prescriptions on food); thus individual staff members might be well-meaning and have liberal attitudes towards minority needs, but are working in an organization which automatically disadvantages black people.
- *Institutional racism:* to all intents and purposes this could be defined in the same way as racism at the organizational level, though we suggest that institutional racism implies a broader definition – an idea that racism subtly permeates the majority culture and all levels of society, causing discrimination to occur in all sorts of unwitting ways. For example, disproportionate numbers of black patients might be referred to certain hospitals in a health authority's district (see, for example, Central Birmingham CHC 1979: 2–6) which, unsurprisingly, are worse resourced than others. More generally, the 'universalist' philosophy of the NHS (the idea that individuals, to be treated equally, must all be treated the same way) may unintentionally disadvantage minority groups.

Our understanding of racism needs to take account of all these levels. But it would be wrong to imply that all older black and Asian patients invariably encounter direct racism or hostility; the problem is deeper than that, and in some cases the friendly and caring attitudes of health service staff compensate for the institutional shortcomings. The evidence on access to health services illustrates this. As Fenton (1986: 50) suggests in relation to the GP service: 'In the main, there is no simple problem of access'. However, as he also notes: 'Access means . . . more than simply getting to the care centre, [it] includes getting satisfactory care as well'.

Going to see a doctor several times, rather than once, may mean that the patient sees the preceding consultations as unsatisfactory or bewildering and has experienced a 'communication gap' with the doctor. McNaught (1984: 24) comments on the evidence that Afro-Caribbean people quite often feel that they must pay for private consultations in order to receive adequate diagnosis or treatment. This suggests that the expectations of at least one minority are not being met by the NHS. Equally, it should not be assumed that increasing numbers of Asian doctors will automatically ease problems of communication with Asian patients – differences of language and social status may be as great or even greater between some Asian patients and an Asian doctor than between the same patients and a doctor of the majority white community.

There will, of course, be genuine cultural misunderstandings between minority patients and their doctors – this is part of a general problem of communication in the consulting room or doctor's surgery (Tuckett *et al.* 1985). And there is some (albeit small) evidence that GPs are becoming aware of ethnicity and language needs when patients present symptoms (Flannery 1981). It also is possible that, in some cases, patients from the Indian subcontinent or from the Caribbean may expect longer consultations than is the norm in Britain, or may wish for more explicit guidance or advice than they receive.

However, the latter view might 'blame the victim' or lay responsibility for communication problems solely at the door of the patient, when the responsibility is shared with the doctor. Research in the United States (Liu 1986) suggests that older people in minority ethnic groups have a firm belief in the value and efficacy of Western medicine. Asian and Afro-Caribbean people in Britain seem to share this belief. Mark Johnson's (1986) research, for example, shows that among Asians in the West Midlands, utilization of alternative Unani and Ayurvedic practitioners is uncommon; almost all Asians are registered with GPs and acceptance of Western medical preventive care, including immunization, is high. At the same time, Johnson found little evidence that patients in minority ethnic groups use their GPs inappropriately.

In the main, therefore, Asian and Afro-Caribbean patients, like the majority, are strongly motivated by the belief that medical therapies will be able to help them, and are constrained by accepted notions of what is 'appropriate' patient behaviour. Despite conforming in these ways, however, black and Asian patients are more likely than their white counterparts to experience dissatisfaction in their dealings with medical practitioners.

Being a patient and receiving medical attention not only involves following specialist advice or being expected to co-operate in being 'worked upon' by practitioners. The patient role also involves learning rules of expected patient behaviour: for example, patients are usually expected to be rational and to explain their symptoms in an appropriate manner, to show pain in appropriate ways, and to comply with medical advice about diet, the therapies being administered, and so on. Medicine may therefore be seen as a social process, involving social rules, values and a culture; it is not simply a set of technical or scientific processes (see also Chapter 8).

It is quite important to grasp the notion that medicine and health services have a social and cultural component. Otherwise, it is all too easy to view medical practitioners as the rational, impartial or 'affectively neutral' actors in relationships with patients, while the patients themselves are pictured as the ones bringing to the encounter emotion, pain, values and particular cultural attitudes – whether they are English, Welsh, Cypriot or Sikh. Yet we know from sociological research (summarized, for example, by Patrick and Scambler 1986) that doctors have been observed to behave quite differently towards patients with the same kinds of medical condition as a result of the doctors' assessments of the social worth, personal behaviour or ethnic group of each patient.

When we reflect on the experience of a Jamaican widow or a Sikh grandfather going into a GP's surgery, or into hospital for treatment, we should therefore remember that it is not a matter of the older black patient bringing an 'awkward' set of expectations or cultural attitudes with him or her. It would be more accurate to see the hospital or medical practitioner culture as exotic and 'awkward', perhaps, in the sense that it demands compliance to rules which are in part culturally defined and unlike the everyday rules of social behaviour. The relationship between patients and medical practitioners always involves some negotiation (Patrick and Scambler 1986: 76).

A key characteristic of the patient role, however, is a certain powerlessness and vulnerability. Some of this comes from the exigencies of the patient's condition, which may involve a lot of pain and fear. But in addition, the relative lack of power experienced by patients is caused by the authority claimed by medical practitioners – their professional rights to do what they consider the best for the patient. While the GP's surgery may not be too intimidating, entry to the hospital often is. When the patient may feel stigmatized or unwanted, or is actually treated as such by hospital staff, the distress and bewilderment which often accompany hospitalization can be doubled.

Personal observation of one hospital in the West Midlands may serve to illustrate some of these points. It is a large general hospital in an inner-city location, close to neighbourhoods in which many Asian and Afro-Caribbean families live. In the reception area on the ground floor – a large, sparsely furnished and uninviting public space – there is a single entrance through which all visitors must pass to go up to the wards. The entrance is barred, however, by a small gate. A notice (in English) forbids any patient to be visited by more than two people at once. A receptionist continually watches the gate and the number of visitors passing through, while in the reception area knots of relatives and friends – Asian, Afro-Caribbean and white – crowd together, waiting their turn to visit patients.

No doubt the decision to restrict the number of visitors on the wards at any one time can be justified on technical or medical grounds: it is an old Victorian hospital and the wards lack space because the addition of modern medical equipment has made them cramped. Perhaps the authorities feared that some patients would be upset by the appearance of large groups of relatives around some beds, especially if racial antagonisms were aroused. On what appear to be 'medical grounds', then (not adding to patients' anxieties), a social norm has been enforced.

Whatever the reasons, however, they are surely debatable. One has the feeling that the hospital 'belongs' to its staff, not to the patients and their visitors. But why should one social definition of the hospital ward be any better than another? Asian patients, for example, may have in their minds a model of hospital care which requires relatives to do a great deal – to visit often, stay with the patients to support them, wash and tend them, and bring food for them. Though this model is born of necessity because nursing care is often inadequate in less industrialized countries, it has some value in a therapeutic sense: it may help to reduce the sense of shock patients feel when hospitalized, and it may reduce post-operative trauma and aid rehabilitation.

In using this example, we do not wish to say that the hospital was necessarily wrong in enforcing its decision to restrict visiting – there are perhaps good reasons, unknown to the authors. However, the impression is given that none of the wider implications of the decision had been considered. One wonders whether patients' or health service consumers' representatives, including people from the minority ethnic communities, had ever been consulted about how visiting by large family groups could be best handled. And bearing in mind the unwelcoming atmosphere of the reception area, why had no attempts been made to inform visitors, in a variety of languages (either in writing or verbally), about the rules on visiting?

As McNaught (1988: 59) observes rather drily, 'The NHS has a poor record for "user friendliness"'. At least some of the problems experienced by black patients in the NHS (reported, for example, by Donovan 1984; Mares *et al.* 1985; Pearson 1986) seem to stem from a general insensitivity to individual needs. Therefore NHS hospitals and other services are not usually predisposed to respond to the needs of black older patients. Though some attempts have been made to improve translation services and communication with Asian patients on arrival at hospital, for example, there is still, according to McNaught (1988: 70), 'a slow development of national race relations policies' by the NHS. Many of the minor improvements described by McNaught (1988: 67) seem to depend on local initiatives and a piecemeal approach; minority ethnic needs do not seem to have been given priority at the higher levels of policy-making.

Ethnic minorities and mental health

According to Littlewood and Lipsedge (1982: 65), the racial bias in institutions has meant failure to diagnose properly in the psychiatric service. They found there to be less use of drugs, more detention in mental hospitals and less use of psychotherapy among ethnic minority groups. While Cochrane and Rowe (1980) found there to be less reported mental illness among Asian immigrants, Henley (1979) argues that this is partly a reflection of stigma (fear about being admitted to hospital), and also a result of lack of understanding among Asians of mental illness and knowledge about available forms of treatment.

Rack (1982: 100) suggests also that linguistic factors affect a person's ability to experience feelings. Manifestations of distress vary across cultures, as does the interpretation of symptoms. Some ethnic groups, whether European, Asian or other, tend to somatize their emotional stress (that is, feel and describe their symptoms in physical terms). Thus a lack of reported mental illness might be due not to migrant resilience but to inadequacies in diagnosis and treatment by health professionals using a European model of medicine.

Furthermore, it could be argued that migration is inherently stressful and leaves lasting scars, leading to exhaustion and fear of movement − feelings which may recur or be reactivated in later life leading to loss, despair, homesickness and anger (Rack 1982: 54–61). To protect against 'culture shock', a term first used by Oberg (1954), some may avoid contact with the outside world, though this cannot go on indefinitely. A non-migrant woman could be insulated for years and then experience the full force of culture shock when the family moves from inner-city enclave to a suburban housing estate. Problems of depression among certain groups of older Asian women were found by Boneham (1987) and evidence of personal anguish and family disruption among refugees is reported by Refugee Action (1987).

To summarize, there has been little research to date specifically on mental illness among older people in Asian and Caribbean communities. However, one interesting project (the Health and Ethnicity Project) being run by the Institute of Human Ageing, Liverpool, is studying levels of depression and senile dementia among older Chinese, Somali, Afro-Caribbean and British black people in the city. Use is being made of an adapted form of a structured questionnaire known as the Geriatric Mental State (GMS), which has been translated into the appropriate languages and applied in interviews in a variety of cultural settings (Copeland 1988). Having identified the incidence and nature of mental health problems among older people in the various communities, the aim is to explore the barriers to the take-up of existing health services and to discuss with the health authority ways of making those services more sensitive to minority needs than they seem to be at present.

The problem of how to manage an ethnically sensitive service to black and Asian dementia sufferers is now with us and will become increasingly important (Norman 1985: 68). As far as older people and mental health in general are concerned, one wonders whether some of the *strengths* of Asian, Caribbean and other cultures' traditional approaches to healing and treatment have been sufficiently recognized. For example, yoga, prayer and spiritual healing offer avenues of therapy which would be familiar to different groups of Asian and Afro-Caribbean people, though of course the introduction of such approaches would have to be managed with sensitivity and knowledge.

In general, the problems experienced by older black people in the health services seem to reflect a basic ethnocentricity and unwillingness to diversify the ways in which patients are treated. Key 'problem areas' (discussed further in Chapter 8) are, first, those of language differences and communication, the provision of translating services, health education in appropriate languages, etc.; second, associated problems stemming from feelings among black patients that they do not receive enough explanation about their stay in hospital, in relation either to their medical treatment or to the social and personal arrangements they need to know about; third, dietary advice by medical practitioners and provision of food in hospital, which all too often seems to make token gestures towards the great variety of different foods eaten by all the ethnic groups in Britain, but which seems to be based on very little understanding of nutrition or of the religious prescriptions affecting some patients' diets; and fourth, a lack of sensitivity to female patients, especially among the Asian communities.

In addition to these problems, which may in part be described as 'structural' or as needing considerable organizational effort to reduce them, there are, however, other problems stemming from direct racial discrimination against black patients. The problems mentioned above, if not completely unintentional (it is always difficult to demonstrate intent, in any case), are caused indirectly through the organizational and social conservatism of the NHS. Direct discrimination, though, is of a different order. McNaught (1988: 59), summarizing evidence from a number of observers, categorizes examples of racial discrimination in terms of: patient handling and reception (for example, 'making racist comments in earshot of the patient'); inadequate explanation or inappropriate treatment during clinical consultation; inadequate advice to patients when consent to medical treatment is sought; 'offhand treatment' and 'unnecessary' or punitive treatment during nursing care; and racist assumptions in medical practitioners' 'behavioural models', which are often 'culture-specific' to white British people.

Conclusion

The health of all older people is a cause for concern. For too long, however, old age and poor health have been seen as synonymous when, in fact, the majority of older people enjoy good health. There is an ever-present danger that old age will be 'medicalized' and seen as a problem in itself.

There are, as Swift (1989: 135) says, 'no grounds for complacency . . . from the point of view of the health consumer'. Obtaining sensitive and good-quality health care is often difficult for the majority of older people, and geriatric medicine has traditionally been a neglected field.

If this is true for the majority, it is even more so for older black people. Most of the problems centre around difficulties in communication and the slowness of the health services to adapt to the realities of a multilingual, multicultural society. Previously adverse employment practices in the NHS and a failure to come to terms with racism partly account for this, as does a general unwillingness to recognize the cultural components in Western medical techniques and approaches to nursing care (Squires 1991). Above all, we conclude that this is still a seriously under-researched area. Much more could be done to monitor the health of Britain's first major cohort of ageing black settlers.

8

Welfare and social services

Introduction

'Social services' and 'welfare' are far from being synonymous terms. Regrettably, however, much of the research on older black people's needs *has* equated welfare with statutory social services, concentrating on how they have been neglected by these services.

But if we think of welfare in a broader sense, it is possible to identify a range of ways in which needs may be met – or again, neglected. Most welfare needs are met by older people themselves, if we include under this heading such things as meals, personal care, companionship and recreation. Relatively few older people ever come into contact with the social services, whether they are among the white majority or in minority ethnic communities. Indeed, there is sometimes a stigma associated with using such services. Negative views about them may be strongly shared by older Asians and Afro-Caribbeans, who have come from countries in which social welfare is associated with basic assistance to the neediest and poorest.

Most 'community' care is actually provided in families, by relatives and spouses, but neighbours and friends also play a small part. It is in just these respects, however, that older black people may be at a disadvantage. They are most clearly disadvantaged in terms of financial resources (see Chapters 2 and 4) and other amenities in the home and, as we have already seen, their families may not be as supportive as is often thought.

Welfare needs may also be met by voluntary organizations or by services offered in the private sector. In this chapter we will examine how far needs are being met in these directions, but especially as far as voluntary organizations are concerned. The role of both sectors should not be underestimated. For example, the British institution of the 'working men's club' can offer cheap and substantial meals to older people as well as to those of working age; other examples include hairdressers who charge low fees for older clients, or bingo halls which provide inexpensive leisure and social contact.

It is quite possible that a number of older black people could also take advantage of these services which lie outside the statutory sector, but there is not much evidence that they are using them on any appreciable scale. And unlike older white people, who are more easily able to exploit their links with established clubs or leisure facilities, older black and Asian people may either feel that such institutions will not meet their needs or, if they did, that they might be made to feel unwelcome; working men's social clubs, for example, have been accused of preventing black people from becoming members. Black and Asian people are not *always* excluded from the facilities used by older white people, but impressionistic evidence suggests that even if they are admitted it is on the terms of the majority – the Afro-Caribbean, Asian or Irish user would be expected to adapt to the ways of the majority.

Given this history, it is not surprising that older migrants to Britain have become increasingly interested in setting up their own voluntary associations, clubs or social centres. Britain's Irish community, for example, shows clearly the vital role of ethnic-specific social clubs. We will discuss below the similarly important role of social and religious centres among the Asian and Afro-Caribbean communities. In some cases these voluntary groups have branched out, becoming providers of community-wide *welfare* services as well as social or recreational centres.

Traditional assumptions about the respective roles of the voluntary and statutory sectors of welfare services in Britain were shaken to the core by Conservative governments bent on reducing the role of social services departments. It is now very unlikely that local authorities will ever again take on the role of providers of services in the way they did before the introduction of legislation on the reform of community care. Minorities face uncertainty about how they will fare under the changed arrangements: the outlook will be discussed at greater length in the second part of this chapter. Before this, however, we need to clarify what is meant by the needs of older black people, how far they have changed or been redefined over recent years, and how social services departments and other agencies have responded to them.

'Their needs are different' – or are they?

When awareness of the needs of older black people in Britain began to grow, the case was often made that these were 'special' or in significant ways different from those of the majority (Blakemore 1983a). There is some truth in this, and we shall discuss minority needs. However, much depends on the level of generality at which needs are defined. Older black people have, like everyone in later life, certain common needs.

Barker (1984), for example, broadly defines the needs of older black people as company, social roles and dignity, adequate housing and financial support. This reminds us that older black people are not some exotic sub-group of society, but share a common humanity with common needs. Barker's view also helps us question the notion that all needs can be met with social services. But even where social services intervention is appropriate, Rowlings (1981) and other commentators on social work with older people have shown how social services departments tend to have rather fixed and limited ideas about what older clients' needs are, often substituting in-depth work with things which are 'done to' the older person: provision of home care, aids and adaptations to the home, and so on.

Different ways of defining 'needs' may help clarify this point (Bradshaw 1972). For example, *felt needs* can be seen as individuals' views about their own needs. Some might be willing to discuss these confidentially – for example in response to a survey – but not want them aired in public or in a family group. *Expressed needs* are those which have been publicly expressed, either as demands by those in need themselves, or by others on their behalf. *Comparative need* is established by comparison between individuals or groups, for example black and white older people, while *normative need* refers to professional definitions of need. The latter definitions raise the enormous question of the validity of outsiders' definitions as against individuals' or clients' own views or wants.

Though it is important to retain the idea that older black people have needs in common with everyone, there is a case for saying that in certain respects their needs may be special or different. Thus many older people – white and black – may have certain religious or spiritual needs, but those of the various Asian and Afro-Caribbean communities will be distinctive in the sense that most people in the majority could be unfamiliar with these needs. The same could be said of diet and food preparation, or aspects of personal care (Squires 1991).

Rather than separating 'special' from 'common' needs, however, we argue that fewer unnecessary or invidious distinctions will be made if we follow Barker's approach. We therefore suggest that four broad kinds of welfare need may be identified, leaving aside health needs which have been discussed in Chapter 7: citizenship needs and rights to welfare; the need for information and awareness of choices; the need for support, when necessary, with activities of daily living; and the need for independence and for relationships beyond the immediate home. Within each type of need there will of course be 'special' needs among particular communities of Afro-Caribbean or Asian people.

Welfare needs – the evidence

Citizenship needs and rights to welfare

As successive immigration laws and Home Office guidance to immigration officials have tightened immigration controls, reducing the flow of migrants from 'black' or New Commonwealth countries, new regulations defining citizenship among people *already* settled in Britain have also been introduced. For example, the 1971 Immigration Act introduced the (now superseded) distinction between 'patrials' and 'non-patrials', while in 1980 the Nationality Act brought in new distinctions and took away the automatic right to citizenship for people born on British soil.

A great deal of anxiety has been generated among black communities about immigration controls and about the ways in which these controls seem to foster racist attitudes towards black and Asian people. We were therefore concerned to find out whether these questions were prominent in the minds of older black people.

Some of the community survey evidence does indicate serious needs in these respects (Berry 1981; Fenton 1986: 27), and reports of comments such as 'We are not welcome in this country' and 'They refused to help me because I am black/Asian' were apparently common, though exactly how widespread is not clear.

The larger-scale community surveys in the Midlands (AFFOR 1981; Coventry 1986) seem to show that a small but significant proportion of older Asians and Afro-Caribbeans mentioned difficulties with immigration or with obtaining social security benefits, or dealing with the Department of Social Security. For example, in Coventry's survey only 2 per cent mentioned immigration problems, though 15 per cent mentioned difficulties with the Department of Social Security. The Birmingham survey also found that only a few expressed worries about similar matters.

These findings should be treated with caution because neither survey set out specifically to examine questions of citizenship or rights to social security; the responses on these subjects were under the heading of 'other problems'. It is arguable that a survey focusing specifically on these questions would uncover needs of a much greater extent.

Alternatively, it could be suggested that older migrants have, for better or worse, resolved any problems of nationality they may have had so that one would naturally expect only a low proportion to be experiencing problems now. While this could be true for the majority, such an assumption can prove to be alarmingly ill founded in certain cases. In one case known to the authors, a retired man from St Vincent discovered that, as St Vincent had become an independent state after the time he had arrived in Britain with an old, now outdated passport, he would in all probability be prevented from settling in Britain upon return from any journey overseas. Unfortunately, this man had no birth certificate with him in Britain and was finding it extremely difficult to arrange for the Vincentian authorities to track it down. Eventually, after years of insecurity and communication between this man and the Vincentian and British authorities, and the intervention of a Member of Parliament, a temporary British passport was eventually replaced by a full British passport.

Observation of the work of any of the community advice centres which provide support to Asian and Afro-Caribbean communities, such as the Asian Resource Centre in Birmingham, confirms that a considerable proportion of their clientele is composed of older people, some of whom will be experiencing problems of nationality or citizenship, as in the case above, as well as others who have problems with claiming the correct level of pension or income support.

The AFFOR (1981) survey showed some time ago that high proportions of older Asians were not receiving a state pension at all – over half of the men and 65 per cent of the women. In nearly every case this will have arisen because many older migrants in the early 1980s had not made sufficient National Insurance contributions to qualify for a full pension. However, some have a right to at least some pension, and may not be aware of this. Over 10 per cent of the AFFOR sample of older Asians reported that they were having difficulties establishing their case for a pension, with uncertainty about their official ages being the main stumbling block. These findings suggest a need for welfare rights workers who have been trained in understanding the particular problems of retired migrant workers and in ways of resolving disputes with the Department of Social Security about birth dates.

Unfortunately, language differences, fears of officialdom, worries about residence rights or just lack of information have all contributed towards substantial under-claiming of other benefits (to compensate for lack of pension). During the interviewing phase (in 1985) of the Coventry survey, for example, numerous enquiries were made by the older Asian respondents about social security benefits they had never heard of. As a result of under-claiming, reported income in households of older black people is appreciably lower than income among older inner-city white people (Bhalla and Blakemore 1981). Certain needs could be inferred from these findings: more accessible and approachable social security officials, translation services, and better targeting of information about social security in media well understood by older black and Asian people.

The need for information and awareness of choices

All the research to date has shown a broad difference between a higher level of knowledge of social services, benefits, and so on, among the Afro-Caribbean community compared with the various Asian communities. It has been suggested that Afro-Caribbeans are not affected by language barriers in the same way as Asians; they have, on the whole, been in Britain longer and are more likely to have made regularized pension arrangements (this is also because greater proportions of Afro-Caribbeans have worked for public sector employers), and for all these reasons they are both more likely to be aware of the welfare system and to claim their benefits than older Asians. Asian women, and particularly the majority who have never been in paid employment, sometimes seem to be outside the welfare system altogether.

This does not mean that Afro-Caribbean people have no problem obtaining benefits or establishing their 'citizenship credentials' – far from it, in some cases. And though there is a broad difference between Asians and Afro-Caribbeans in terms of their needs for information, it should be emphasized that older Afro-Caribbeans also have needs – though of a different nature. First, all the research has worked with a very basic definition of how well informed older black people are about social services. The question usually asked is whether they have heard about mobile meals, home care, and the like. But respondents would only need the vaguest idea to be able to respond positively to this question. Therefore, although in one survey (Bhalla and Blakemore 1981) older Afro-Caribbeans appeared to be only a little less well informed than older whites, one wonders whether services and benefits are that widely known.

Second, awareness could imply that, if in need, older Afro-Caribbean people would choose to use services. However, the dignity of a number of older Afro-Caribbeans was offended by their experiences in Britain in the 1950s and

Table 8.1   Knowledge of social services among Afro-Caribbean and Asian older people (percentages)

Services	Coventry[1]		Birmingham[2]			
	Asians	Afro-Caribbeans	Asians		Afro-Caribbeans	
			Males	Females	Males	Females
Heard of:						
Day centre	46	94	18	5	54	63
Home Help	16	86	22	13	78	86
Sheltered housing	11	63	–	–	–	–
Old people's homes	7	87	40	19	84	92
Mobile meals	14	87	15	10	71	86
Lunch clubs	5	80	7	3	32	38
Home visiting/ nightwatch	–	–	12	10	53	60

[1] Coventry (1986)
[2] AFFOR (1981)

1960s (see Chapter 5). Consequently there is still some distrust of apparently exclusive or discriminatory 'white' organizations, which social services departments seem to represent.

In examining the findings in Table 8.1, the need of older Asian people for very basic information is immediately apparent. But following on from our discussion of the Afro-Caribbeans, these data should not lead to the conclusion that the Caribbean community have no need for a more sensitive approach than at present. Substantial proportions of Afro-Caribbean men, for example, seem to be unaware of certain domiciliary services.

What do older Asian and Afro-Caribbean people themselves feel their needs are? This was a difficult question for many older Asians, and especially women, as often the first person to discuss the range of social services with them was an interviewer for one of the community surveys.

Only the Coventry survey systematically compared actual use of various services with felt need (see Table 8.2). Bearing in mind that a considerable number of older Asians would have been hazy about what each service actually entailed, these data indicate a substantial amount of interest among them. We should also remember that only a minority of older *white* people at any one time would regard these services as appropriate to their needs.

As we discussed in Chapter 6, there is a marked difference between the needs of men and women in Asian communities, both in terms of levels of awareness (see Table 8.1) and in relation to felt needs. For example, in the AFFOR survey 45 per cent of older Asian men expressed a strong interest in going to a day centre if it could be sited locally, but only 18 per cent of Asian women said they would – or could – go.

Where Asian day centres or social clubs were available locally, the Birmingham respondents were additionally asked why they did not want to

Table 8.2 Current use of and interest in social services (Coventry)[1] (percentages)

Service	Currently used	Not interested	Interested, with provisos	Don't know
Day centres	6.0	41.0	44.0[2]	9.0
Home help	1.5	72.0	11.6[3]	14.9
Sheltered housing	0.5	80.0	12.0	7.5
Old people's homes	0.2	91.0	8.3[4]	0.5
Mobile meals	0.2	60.0	30.3[5]	9.5
Lunch clubs	1.6	80.0	18.0[6]	0.4

[1] Unpublished data, Coventry Social Services (1986)
[2] Interested if local (30%); if no smoking (6%); if sexes separated (4%); if own religious/ethnic group only (4%)
[3] Asian or Afro-Caribbean home helps preferred
[4] Interested for possible future use (8%); interested now (0.3%)
[5] Non-vegetarian halal meals (5%); non-vegetarian, no beef (11.3%); vegetarian (14%)
[6] Interested for possible future use (14.0%); interested now, depending on nature of food (4%)

attend. Illness or physical inability was mentioned by a few, but language barriers and fears of not being welcome were mentioned by a fifth of the women and a third of the men. However, the majority of non-attenders gave no reason other than they felt they had no particular need to use a social centre. For most of these older Asians, such preferences are perfectly natural – after all, only a minority of the white elderly population opt to use day centres or other services. However, as Boneham's research shows, there are hidden needs among older Asian women. Some cannot easily express their needs and, even if they do, may be unaware of how needs for company and support could be met outside their family. Though older Asian women can be restricted by traditional family roles and expectations, these barriers can be overcome: transport from the home to a social centre is a vital factor, for example.

The research also suggests that involving women in developing their own services and support systems is highly important. However, to get initiatives off the ground there may well be need for leadership from others. For example, in Birmingham very few older Asian women felt they would be able to organize their own activities or services – in contrast to the men, two-fifths of whom expressed a strong interest in lending help to any initiative from their own ranks (AFFOR 1981). For older Asian women, then, there is a problem of community development: intervention is needed but could stifle initiative.

To sum up, older black people, especially older Asians, are lamentably ill informed about their welfare rights and the social services. Positive action is required by social services departments and other organizations to increase awareness.

Provision itself can have a dramatic effect on the awareness and expression of need. For example, before the first sheltered housing schemes for older Asians were opened in Birmingham, Leicester and elsewhere, not many Asians seemed to be aware of, or interested in, sheltered housing. It was assumed that older Asians wished to remain with their families. But once the sheltered housing schemes opened, their managers were deluged with applications. This shows that elaborate surveys to demonstrate need are not always necessary. The provision of a service or facility – as long as some preliminary estimate of need and suitability is made – can act as a demonstration of further needs and quickly becomes a talking point in the black community.

The need for support with activities of daily living

Among older black and Asian people this need – for example, help with cooking, cleaning the house, shopping – is relatively low, but will grow as the 'migrant cohort' ages. In a medium-sized city such as Coventry there are about a quarter of a million inhabitants, 10–15 per cent of whom are of Asian or Afro-Caribbean descent. The comprehensive survey conducted by the city (Coventry 1986) showed that 137 older people were experiencing difficulties with one or more important tasks of daily life (Table 8.3), and this represented about one in ten of the older Asian and black population in Coventry. A similar picture emerged in the earlier survey in Birmingham (AFFOR 1981), where rates of illness – particularly among older Afro-Caribbean women appeared to be high (see Chapter 7). The data in Table 8.3 are based on self-reported problems or needs, but given the modest expectations of older Asians and Afro-Caribbeans they are as likely to underestimate as overestimate need.

Though all but a few of those in need of help live with relatives it is worth underlining the plight of the minority living alone. It is these people who, if they become frail, are almost forced to use whatever social services are available – whether or not they have been adapted to suit different religious or ethnic needs. Having to come to terms with uncomprehending 'carers' and, however well meaning, the provision of food or home care which violates familiar and well-respected values and norms, can be a tremendous shock to an older person used to caring for him/herself.

The need for independence and relationships beyond the home

Barker (1984) identified a common need for 'roles and dignity', which arguably comes close to concepts of independence and the freedom to make relationships on one's own terms. Even if an older person finds it difficult or impossible to get out of the house, it should still be possible to find ways of maintaining or enhancing that person's links with the neighbourhood and wider community – being able to choose one's own food, for example, or keeping in touch with one's religious community, or being able to communicate with relatives and friends. Above all, there is both a right and a need to make choices in old age.

Establishing how far older black people have needs which are unmet in this sphere is, however, a more difficult matter. Defining independence involves cultural values. And it is not always clear who should be responsible for meeting these needs: what right or responsibility does a statutory or voluntary organization have to intervene?

While older Asian women, for example, are sometimes able to control their destiny within the context of traditional family structures, Boneham's and

Table 8.3 Difficulties with daily living among Asian and Afro-Caribbean older people in Coventry, by living arrangements (percentages)

	Alone	*Living:*		*Total*	*N*
		With spouse only	*With spouse and relatives/others*		
Some/all activities[1]					
difficult	0.9	0.9	9.3	11.1	137
None difficult	3.1	16.2	69.6	88.9	1,097
Total	4.0	17.1	78.9	100.0	1,234 [2]

Source: unpublished data, Coventry (1986)

[1] The survey enquired about mobility, cooking, cleaning home and collecting pension.
[2] The survey total was estimated to represent approximately two-thirds of the total Coventry population of older Asian and Afro-Caribbean people.

others' studies have pinpointed various needs for greater independence and choice. These might be summarized as having more self-determination in three main areas of life. The first is control over their present and future income, and having greater financial security – some older Asian women, for example, 'voluntarily' pool their income with that of the household. Some are badly in need of advice on pensions, housing rights, and making a will. A second area of need is in terms of health problems and the management of chronic conditions – many older women are not made aware of how services could be better co-ordinated to help them. And thirdly, depression and loneliness could be counteracted by easier access to the company of equals or a friendly social circle which enables them to escape from the confines of the home.

On the whole older Asian women have the greater need in these spheres, though older Asian men also have needs for greater independence and relationships outside the home. As with the women, it is vitally important that the older people themselves play a part in defining what their needs are; otherwise, well-meaning but inappropriate interventions could offend by working against traditional norms and expectations. For example, is it right to expect older Asian men to view old age as a category somewhat separated off from other age groups? Do older Asian men expect or need 'old people's' services or facilities? The evidence would seem to suggest that preferences among older Asian men are often for mixed-age groups in which to extend their friendships and social ties (Blakemore 1985b; NISW 1990: 42), though there may also be needs for groups or social arenas in which older people predominate. However, older Asian men have expressed their needs to a far greater extent than women either by publicly demonstrating that they are at a 'loose end', wandering through streets and parks (see Chapter 6), or by helping to set up informal meeting places or clubs.

Finally, the evidence on need for support and companionship indicates a broad difference between older Asians and Afro-Caribbeans. Though the support given by extended families to older Asians can be exaggerated, it does play a significant part. Older Afro-Caribbeans, many of whom are living in couples or alone, are more likely to need support by social services or community groups and are also more likely to express their needs. However, there is a considerable amount of unrecognized and *felt* need among the Asian communities, and especially among older Asian women.

Needs met?

In the changing climate of social services provision, in which voluntary and private agencies will increasingly become the main providers and the statutory sector will perform the roles of assessing, managing and purchasing, the chances of social services departments directly providing anything to older black people will become even more remote than before. But it is important to remember that nothing much was *ever* provided; from the beginning, the pattern was for the voluntary sector to initiate services specifically for older black people (Blakemore 1985b; Norman 1985; Patel 1990).

It would be wrong, however, to suggest that all local authorities have been completely uninterested in the question of meeting the needs of older black people. Some have shown considerable interest and, among some individual employees, there has been a willingness to consider minority needs. But Connelly (1989), Patel (1990) and others have noted persistent obstacles to greater social services involvement. These problems include:

1 'One-off' commitments – a local authority is unable or unwilling to commit funds on a permanent basis, but might release a small amount of money, for example, to assist with recruiting Asian home helps. Even for 'one-off' commitments the social services department might cast about for additional funds from elsewhere. For example, the thorough and large-scale survey in Coventry (1986) was mainly funded by the then Manpower Services Commission.

2 Using exising staff – these may be resourceful, but are commonly overstretched and undertrained, especially in the field of caring for older people. Are they the right people to do the job? Distinctive cultural needs, ability to communicate easily with older black and Asian people and problems of racism among white staff support the case for the employment of black and Asian staff, yet according to Connelly (1989) progress in this direction was slow until recently.

3 Using existing resources or facilities – this may be unavoidable because of tightly constrained social services budgets, but can prevent experimentation. Social services departments have been very unwilling to create new budget headings for expenditure on 'minority' projects. 'Lending' a minibus or a meeting room to a group can be managed more easily under existing budgets. Thus, social services departments have been forced to act in a half-hearted way towards black community organizations, underlining the marginal status of minority projects.

4 A record of failure – especially in a particular service such as mobile meals. In both Birmingham and Wolverhampton, for example, the city-run 'meals on wheels' services tried to cater for the Asian and

Afro-Caribbean communities, but met with little success in terms of take-up. Some local authorites have had a degree of success in supporting new services for older black people, but, as we suggested, they are few and far between.

The provision of food stands out as an area in which partnerships between local authorities and each major community group are the most effective way of meeting needs. But there are other areas – admittedly involving high capital expenditure, as in the case of local authority sheltered housing – in which a leading local authority role would probably have met with more success. The focus of some local authorities on meals provision perhaps occurred because it initially seemed easy to 'tack on' additional 'special diets' to a service already geared to the notion of special needs. Mobile meals providers often have a concept of 'Asian' meals, perhaps thinking of them as a variant of 'vegetarian meals'. Thus the idea of special needs had penetrated, but in a rather clumsy way; in areas such as day centres, sheltered housing and home care, the concept of special needs may not be recognized at all.

Why have social services departments generally failed to become genuinely multicultural? Patel (1990), Connelly (1989) and others suggest institutional racism is the root cause. However, there are also features of social services organization which are not specifically racist but which have adversely affected older black people.

First, meeting distinctive needs has always been problematic for the statutory sector because of an underlying philosophy of universalism. This is a policy of providing a common set of services for everyone, or 'treating individuals in like fashion'. It assumes that a basic fairness will prevail if no special treatment is given to any particular individuals or groups.

In race relations, universalism becomes a 'colour-blind' approach (Patel 1990). Black and white will be treated in exactly the same way and it is assumed to be wrong to develop special approaches to either. But it is also assumed that the burden of change must lie with the user rather than the provider of services: the 'immigrant' must be prepared to 'integrate' or adapt to the ways of the host country.

A basic flaw in universalistic and colour-blind philosophies is that established social services can never treat individuals in like fashion if they are imbued with the culture and values of one group, white service providers and welfare professionals. The idea that social services are, or should be, culturally neutral is therefore questionable. Also, the view that low take-up of a service is always something to do with the nature of the clientele can lead to a 'customer is always wrong' perspective: customers have irritating habits such as being different from each other, or having a different culture from the management.

Defined more imaginatively, equality means treating individuals and groups sensitively, and sometimes differently, in order to achieve similar outcomes (for example, receiving home care, entering sheltered housing). From this point of view, the plight of older black people only illustrates a much wider problem with statutory social services. Meeting their needs, far from detracting from the services received by the majority, may actually help improve the sensitivity of the providers and the organization as a whole.

However, there are occasions when redressing the historic disadvantages of black people *will* appear to be favouring the minority. To take local authority sheltered housing as an example, we typically find that no attempts have been made to prioritize applications on grounds of race or ethnicity, and very rarely have older black people been offered council accommodation together, in a single sheltered housing site within a convenient or nearby inner-city neighbourhood. More often – as in Birmingham, for example – older black people in need of sheltered housing were offered places in suburban sites, sometimes distant from relatives, friends, familiar shops and religious centres. They usually turned down such offers, according to the reports and experience of Anil Bhalla, a long-standing community worker and manager of Handworth's Asian Resource Centre.

Giving older black people priority or even building new housing schemes for them would not be 'positive discrimination', according to Edwards's (1987) definition, because it would simply be responding to greater need. However, such an approach would be seen as running against the political grain by appearing to be an example of 'favouritism' to minority groups.

Defending their stance, social services managers have sometimes argued that the development of distinctive 'Asian', 'Afro-Caribbean' and 'European' accommodation or services would only pave the way towards a new kind of apartheid. Perhaps there are grounds for these fears, and there are cases of successful racial integration of residential accommodation and day care – for example, the Narvijan project at Preston Lodge in Leicester. However, such concerns sit oddly with an acceptance of all-white old people's homes and sheltered housing schemes in the suburbs – if they are exclusively white, why should an all-Asian or all-Afro-Caribbean residential scheme be problematic? However, targeting a housing scheme or a social service to a minority does not mean that it need become racially exclusive, and an old people's home specializing in meeting the needs of older Afro-Caribbeans, for example, could also admit others from different ethnic backgrounds.

The voluntary sector

A few years before this publication, one author reviewed the progress of a range of voluntary sector or community groups in meeting the welfare needs of older Asian and Afro-Caribbean people (Blakemore 1985b); another survey, by Norman (1985), was also published at the same time.

Both these surveys now seem to have been in some ways too pessimistic, but in others perhaps justifiably so. The over-pessimistic conclusions were that a majority of the small voluntary groups would disappear. This has not happened, and there is a fairly extensive and growing network of older people's social or day centres, meals services, and home and hospital visiting services in the major British cities. However, neither report was too pessimistic in anticipating continuing difficulties in obtaining permanent funding, or adequate staffing and premises. The number of voluntary schemes may be relatively stable, or even growing, but this masks a proportion of services and centres which are reduced or closed each year, to be replaced by other short-lived projects. The survivors must face the continual head applying for renewal of funds and lobbying for support from all quarters.

Before discussing the problems, however, it is worth focusing on strengths. This is important for two reasons: first, because 'community' care policies will place increasing reliance upon voluntary providers; and second, because Asian and Afro-Caribbean community groups have now gained many years' experience in developing services for older black people. It would be a pity if their contribution were to be pushed to the sidelines by the bigger, white-dominated voluntary organizations as they win contracts from purchasing authorities to provide services.

For readers not familiar with the earlier studies of black and Asian voluntary groups caring for older people, it should be noted that the survey to which we refer (Blakemore 1985b) drew information from a total of 48 projects, some of which were described by Norman (1985); 28 projects were for older Asian people and 20 for older Afro-Caribbeans. The achievements and value of these projects may be summarized under the following headings:

Independent and responsive?
Most projects are fairly small and cater for between 20 and 50 older people. They have not become large-scale, unresponsive organizations in the way that some larger charities do (Brenton 1985). A substantial number of services for older people have grown organically from existing or 'parent' associations among the Asian and Afro-Caribbean communities. They have not been imposed by outsiders and have usually been developed to respond to a well-known need within the community for social support or practical help. Despite funding problems, all these projects therefore enjoy a degree of independence; they are not yet creatures of social services departments and have the advantages of flexibility and knowing best how to meet needs.

Participation?
As the older population of Afro-Caribbeans and Asians will be a 'young old' group for the foreseeable future, it is quite common to find that users of the services play a major part in providing them, or at least in effectively advising what they want. The role of Afro-Caribbean women has already been mentioned, but in projects for Asian people the older men also appear to participate fully in deciding what goes on. Where Asian women are fortunate enough to have their own groups they too will play a big part, though their role needs to be advanced.

Multifunctional?
Some of the projects we surveyed were able to offer only a limited range of activities or services. However, it is a hallmark of the bigger and more successful projects that a range of valuable services has been brought together quite imaginatively. For example, Norman (1985) cites a number of Afro-Caribbean day centres and social clubs, some of which combine meals provision with educational and craft classes, holidays and visits to places of interest, home and hospital visiting circles, and opportunities to see health workers and therapists such as chiropodists. Sometimes the multifunctional

nature of a project develops in an unplanned way: for example, a Birmingham Social Services Department project to help Asian stroke sufferers developed additionally into a social circle or club for carers of the stroke victims.

If British or Western preconceptions of services are laid aside, less specialized activities or functions can develop. For example, the whole notion of services restricted to older people may be questioned. The survey of voluntary projects found that a third of the Asians' and a quarter of the Afro-Caribbeans' schemes did not restrict services to older people. We have found examples of middle-aged Asians sharing day centres with their older counterparts and of Afro-Caribbean meals services being extended to younger Afro-Caribbean disabled people (Blakemore 1985b).

Inclusive?

There is always a danger, if voluntary organizations are based on ethnic or religious communities, that the services they provide will be restricted to members of the organization's community. But the earlier findings showed that neither the various Asian projects nor those in the Afro-Caribbean community are particularly exclusive (Blakemore 1985b). The most specialized projects were among Pakistani Muslim communities – six were sampled and they rarely included non-Muslim users. However, all the other projects included mix of ethnic groups, to a greater or lesser extent. Among Afro-Caribbean projects it was possible to find older white people from a variety of ethnic backgrounds using the services from time to time. In Birmingham, for example, a community group helping older and younger Afro-Caribbeans to recover from mental illnesses also welcomed white people who wished to eat there or to join in a range of social and therapeutic activities.

Against considerable odds, therefore, the hard work of people in Asian and Afro-Caribbean communities has established a number of voluntary social services which can be of great benefit to older people. However, it is no comment on the efforts of the organizers to say that the voluntary system also suffers from a number of disadvantages; indeed, many of these drawbacks, such as lack of funding, are only too well known to the organizations themselves. There is little doubt that the voluntary sector is the most effective in meeting most of the needs of older people in minority ethnic communities because of the advantages listed above. However, the following problems need urgent attention:

Funding

This is perhaps the most central problem. It is not just a problem of inadequate amounts of money, but also a series of problems associated with the system of financing agencies: temporary or annual funding inhibits sensible planning and the ability to build up experienced staff; experienced staff may spend more time chasing fund applications than in delivering or developing services; and dependence on a variety of fund or grant sources may mean that one project may have to try to meet the criteria of quite different and separate organizations – for example, a charity, a social services department and the Employment Agency.

Should religious organizations become part of the 'community care' based welfare system?
Photograph: Abdullah Badwi

Where social services department funding for a post is involved, the money may have been made available as a result of the local authority claiming it under Section 11 of the 1966 Local Government Act. As Norman (1985: 141) points out, Section 11 funding of posts is a mixed blessing – it is a valuable source of extra funding, but adds to the instability of staffing community groups and helps local authorities avoid a full financial commitment to meeting the needs of older black people.

In 1985 the survey of voluntary groups revealed the impact of lack of funds on the quality of services and facilities available: all too often services had to be provided in accommodation either too cramped or too large, with inadequate heating and furniture, and with temporary or part-time staff who have had little or no opportunities for training.

Patchiness
This is often a problem when voluntarism becomes the main principle behind welfare provision: sometimes there may be problems of overlap and duplication, though this is very unlikely at this stage of development in services for older black people. More worryingly, a voluntary system is almost bound to lead to neglect of certain categories of older people. For example, those who are not well integrated in their own community or who have rejected religious affiliations – or been rejected by the religious-minded – may find that they are left out in the cold.

While ethnic exclusivity is not yet a problem among the voluntary projects already established, there is no doubt that some ethnic communities are proving to be more successful in setting up projects than others. In a voluntary system it is only to be expected that communities with greater resources – money, education, professional members and contacts – will be able to establish good community centres and support systems for their older members. The older Asians who have lived in East Africa, for example, have been able to set up some of the most ambitious programmes and services for older people, including anything from meals at a neighbourhood centre to holidays in Europe and Africa. Bangladeshi communities, on the other hand, are relatively poorer, have fewer professional representatives or advocates and in any case form a smaller community. These differences raise the question of how far local authorities should intervene, or are able to intervene, to address problems of patchiness of provision.

Inequalities
These arise *within* voluntary forms of provision, adding to the ethnic inequalities discussed above. Voluntary organizations usually mirror the communities in which they are based and are very likely to perpetuate the community's hierarchy. As noted in Chapters 5 and 6, there are class and status distinctions among both the Afro-Caribbean and Asian communities and, as with the white majority, they will have some impact on the ability of different groups to use services. However, we do not yet know what effects there may be and whether, for example, caste distinctions play much of a part in shaping attitudes to a community project or social centre. For example, do higher-status older people feel that such services are 'beneath them', much as a

middle-class white person might be reluctant to mix in a 'working-class' older people's day centre?

We do know that gender inequality is a marked feature of Asian voluntary projects (Blakemore 1985b). Most of the services to older Asians are provided by men and used by men. Only three out of 26 Asian projects sampled were used exclusively by women, and another five (mainly East African Asian) were used approximately equally by men and women.

It should be stressed, of course, that such gender inequalities are not simply a feature of the voluntary nature of the Asians' projects; the sharp gender divisions in social life in the various Asian communities would presumably have an effect whether services were in the statutory or independent sector. The evidence from Afro-Caribbean projects shows that gender inequality in access and patterns of use is not an issue. However, the problem of tackling gender inequality in autonomous or semi-independent organizations does raise sensitive political questions. As we noted in 1985, many of the organizers of Asian voluntary projects were beginning to deal with the problem of underuse of services by Asian women, and given this openness and readiness to discuss gender inequalities it would seem important for others in the field to continue to raise questions.

Older people, carers and 'professionals' – face-to-face

While our primary aim has not been to produce a step-by-step practical guide, especially as several publications already provide useful advice (see, for example, Henley 1979; Mares *et al.* 1985; Squires 1991), we have been struck by the relatively undeveloped state of discussion about the quality of relationships between black older people, carers and service providers, or how mutual understanding might be improved.

A number of informative reports give accounts of developments in voluntary services, or problems and shortfalls in care, but the way older people perceive and respond to these services is mostly discussed in generalities – one has to scour such reports for occasional insights into what makes them work at a personal level, or what may be going wrong (see, for example, Daniel 1988; Gilbert 1988; Darby 1989; McFarland *et al.* 1989; *Social Work Today* 1990; Pharoah and Redmond 1991).

There is also an understandable reluctance among many in the minority communities to involve themselves in what might boil down to giving 'cultural tips' on getting on with older black and Asian people. Such detailed 'tips' on practice can be highly stereotyping and misleading: first, they may over-generalize ('Hindus never eat meat', 'Sikhs never drink alcohol', and so on); and second, they may abstract particular cultural traits or preferences from a more general understanding of the history and culture of a community. Dietary restrictions, for example, are not examples of eccentricity or fads but are an integral part of ways of life. Food has a deep social or philosophical significance. Usually, food categories are shaped by religion, but even where dietary restrictions are not based on religious prescriptions 'taboo' foods are well known (many people in Britain, for instance, find the idea of eating horse meat abhorrent).

Continuing with the example of diet, the National Extension College's (1986: 2) guidelines on 'Health and Race' sensibly combine basic information with the advice that

> Individuals vary: *it is always necessary to ask and never assume that these rules are followed by all individuals.* If possible check in advance whether there are certain foods that a person does not wish to eat, or certain times when they will want to fast, for example during . . . Ramadan . . .

The first and most important practical advice therefore seems to be: develop an open-minded approach, question assumptions, explore sensitive ways of asking what older people themselves want. A search for 'ethnic tips on how to behave' may actually work against this reflective approach, especially if it leads practitioners into thinking that they cannot apply general principles or techniques to older people in minority communities.

Cameron *et al.* (1989) show that district nurses in their survey had made little attempt to learn from older black and Asian patients. For example, none had encouraged older people to discuss their life histories. This raises the question of whether district nurses have had the opportunity to gain background knowledge of minority communities – without this they perhaps would not fully realize the significance of particular events in individuals' lives. However, the example does challenge the assumption that service providers and professionals should always be the advisers or imparters of information, never the listeners: a shortcoming which bedevils social work with older people in general (Rowlings 1981).

In the summary of advice and information on face-to-face relationships which follows, we are therefore hoping that it will be received as a summary of options or insights for 'reflective practitioners' rather than as a list of specific do's and don'ts. As older people in minority ethnic groups form a heterogeneous and rapidly changing population, there are no absolutely firm guidelines. To give some structure, however, the following advice – which others working in the field have put forward – is grouped under three headings: making contact and beginning a relationship; developing a relationship; evaluating relationships and outcomes. Much of the practical advice applies to all three stages or kinds of relationship, though the 'career' concept helps show how certain skills and understandings are crucial at some points, perhaps less so at others.

Making contact

Examples of this phase or type of relationship could be: a hospital or health centre receptionist registering an older black or Asian patient, a social worker or clerical assistant working on 'intake' duty, a health visitor or district nurse making his or her first call to a client's/patient's home, or a home care organizer arranging to assess a client's needs. A number of points spring to mind in connection with such situations.

Names

There is nothing more unsettling, especially if one is going through a stressful time, than for someone who is in a position of authority or a 'gatekeeper' role consistently to mispronounce, mishear, forget or struggle with names. Now that some regional health authorities and certain publications (for example, Henley 1979) provide guides and practical exercises on the main naming systems among South Asian, Chinese and other communities, there is no excuse for any authority or employer to shirk the responsibility of providing training for receptionists, professionals and others in these respects.

Names also provide vital information on the ethnic identity and, in all probability, the religious affiliation and needs of a client or service user – though, as will be recalled, it is of crucial importance to check whether such assumptions are correct. Someone's name may appear to indicate a certain ethnic, national or religious background, but is this right?

As all the practical advice points out, getting names right at the beginning helps establish rapport and ensures that the correct people are seen, or registered, or have their cases assessed. Such is the confusion about Asian naming systems in some of the health and welfare services that the wrong people may be interviewed or visited, while someone who is patiently queueing does not respond when his/her names are called out in the wrong order. For instance, while the Hindu system of personal, second and subcaste names fits reasonably well into the traditional British system, the Muslim naming system does not: the first 'title' name among men (for example, Mohammed) is not to be used as a 'first' or personal name. It is acceptable to use a second, personal name as a surname, but that name will not be shared by a family group; to deal appropriately with this, Henley (1979: 96) demonstrates how a Muslim family's names can be recorded as a group. Above all, the very last thing a social services or health worker should do is attempt to verify names by asking to see passports or official documents such as pension books or social security documents. This will immediately cast the welfare practitioner in the role of immigration official or some other representative of officialdom. Barriers to further communication will be erected and it will be extremely difficult to win co-operation if this happens.

What day/date is it?
You may have arranged to meet the relatives of an older person on a particular day, but find that they do not turn up. Or you may not be aware, until you arrive unexpectedly to visit the family, that it is a special day. Making appointments should be carried out with some awareness of days of religious observance, the major festival days and phases of the year which have special significance (see Henley 1979, and contact local community leaders for information). Again, however, the underlying principle of asking the client or older person is the most important. A Friday appointment is not necessarily going to be ruled out by someone who is a Muslim, and a family may be delighted to invite an outsider to their home on a festival day: showing awareness is the key.

Non-verbal communication
Body posture, facial expression, eye contact, physical contact and distance, and so on, are always important, but particularly so when people meet for the first time. The practical advice given by Henley and Mares *et al.* seems to be centred

upon two main observations: first, in a cross-cultural exchange the 'Western' or white British practitioner should not be afraid to show reassurance and concern. When people are going through a difficult time, for example, it is probably better to cry, or smile or demonstrate kindness than to try to force a deadpan expression for fear of breaking some imagined cultural taboo. However, it is also important to learn the basic truth that non-verbal signals mean different things in different cultures. As Mares *et al.* (1985: 61) observe:

> In some cultures 'yes' is indicated by nodding the head, in others by shaking it. Movements and gestures . . . can have very different meanings. In some cultures it is unacceptable for members of the same sex to touch each other in public; in others it is unacceptable for members of the opposite sex to do so. Comfortable physical distance between speakers varies . . . as does the degree of eye contact . . . If possible, always check . . . any judgements you make with the person concerned or with other people from his/her community.

Building up awareness of these conventions is highly important for practitioners if they are to avoid upsetting or demeaning older people. This is good practice whatever ethnic group is involved. Traditional British culture attaches great significance to the politenesses of life, for example, and older white people may grow upset if carers are too demonstrative or 'gushing', or use their first names rather than the preferred 'Mrs Jones' or 'Mr Smith'. However, a white practitioner might decide to compensate for the apparent stiffness and undemonstrativeness of British culture by embracing, holding hands or giving other physical reassurance to an older Indian person who is going into hospital or has experienced a bereavement. Yet such physical contact, given for the best of intentions, might cause the recipient considerable difficulty. A moment's thought, a simple question, or some other check would establish if this were the case, or whether physical reassurance is indeed appropriate.

Awareness of non-verbal cues is also highly important for the practitioner to be able to assess his/her impact upon the older person and family at home. McCalman (1990) brings out particularly well the problems that may be encountered when trying to establish a trusting relationship with Asian family carers. Intervention by outsiders in family matters may well be seen as a disgrace, especially if the older people have previously been living apart from the larger family group.

Practitioners will need to tread very carefully in order to build trust and confidence in such situations, and an understanding of the reasons for relatives' reluctance to share information is vital in this.

Developing a relationship

Many personal contacts between black and Asian older people and welfare practitioners, assistants and reception staff are limited to brief encounters, but a proportion become longer-lasting relationships. Older people in minority groups confront the possibility that such relationships will continue to stumble along, dogged by misunderstandings, the difficulty of language barriers and coolness or even hostility.

Mares *et al.* (1985: 63) make a telling point, based on research on nursing, about the perceived popularity or unpopularity of different kinds of patient. Nurses' enjoyment of their work has less to do with patients' needs or the nature of their illnesses than patients' attitudes to treatment, their friendliness and sense of humour. Patients who know nurses' names and are able to communicate readily are the most highly valued. Patients who are unable to communicate readily, and especially those who do not speak much English, will be at a considerable disadvantage in trying to establish themselves as 'good' patients. But there is more to this problem than language: for example, cultural attitudes to health, illness and the task of 'getting better' may vary significantly. Joking about a serious illness, or trying to make light of it, may be highly valued in one culture but not another. And there is also the issue of racial discrimination: older black people's lack of confidence in service providers or anticipation of racist attitudes may make it difficult for them to play the 'good patient' or 'good resident/client' role (see Chapter 7).

As a considerable number of older minority-group patients and service users are at a disadvantage, it is up to the practitioners and professionals to begin to build bridges and to move relationships beyond the rather limited or stilted exchanges that often take place. There are several major aspects to this.

Language use

This raises a number of important issues which we now discuss in brief.

Though nothing can compensate for the presence of a fluent speaker of one's own language during times of need, there is an argument for familiarizing practitioners from the majority community with key words – greetings, goodbyes, politenesses, and terms relating to health, welfare and family – in the minority language(s) they come across in their work (Mares *et al.* 1985: 73). Though it is difficult to learn even the basic elements of a language and mistakes can be made, such efforts are almost always rewarded: it can be a considerable boost, if one is in a minority ethnic group, to find that someone in authority cares enough to have at least tried to learn one's language. This should not substitute for policies to encourage the employment of minority language speakers by health and social services providers. However, local authorities do provide accessible courses in Asian and other minority languages and, even if a working knowledge is not attained, there may still be considerable value in practitioners compiling lists of key words to carry with them.

A second issue concerns the need for practical advice on use of English with those for whom it is a second language. Thinking how we use English with those who have a limited knowledge of it has valuable 'spin-off' effects for majority older people as well as those in the minority communities. Demeaning or condescending expressions stand out sharply when they are addressed to older black people, but they are reflections of a wider problem of an unthinking approach to the way we communicate. For care staff to call a white older person a 'naughty girl' may be bad enough because of its infantilizing effect, but to someone who does not speak much English it might sound particularly serious or harsh. And the need for practitioners to 'check back', to determine whether they have been understood by someone who does not speak English as a first language, suggests valuable lessons for practice with all older people.

Among other advice, Mares *et al.* (1985) and Henley (1979) suggest the following about uses of English:

• find simple but effective ways of checking that you have been understood (avoiding, for example, questions which prompt the response 'yes');
• listen to the client's/patient's own use of English and try to use words within his/her vocabulary;
• avoid idioms, and exercise care in the use of examples or analogies, which are often culture-bound;
• simplify sentences, but do not use 'pidgin' English – as Mares *et al.* (1985:67) explain: 'Simplifying is not the same as condensing. If you condense what you say, you make it *more* . . . difficult to understand. A longer simplified explanation is easier to follow than a condensed one'.

A third issue is the need for other communication skills in addition to language. People in minority linguistic groups, and especially older people, often lack confidence and feel very nervous about using the English they do have. Such fears of being scorned or misunderstood are compounded when older people are going through a life crisis or experiencing illness, as they often are at the point they come into contact with health and social services practitioners.

The practical guide to better communication by Mares *et al.* suggests sensible ways of complementing language skills by trying to reduce the sources of stress and uncertainty in minority patients'/clients' encounters with practitioners: for example, more time should be allowed for interviews if the first languages of the practitioner and client are not the same; long silences should be avoided (for example, when a social services worker completes a form, or a nurse performs a clinical task); stress is reduced if clients and their families see the same staff, rather than a bewildering succession of different names and faces; and clients may appreciate being given written information (or notes and drawings, in the case of medical advice) to take away with them. Even if it is in English, such information can be translated later by friends or relatives.

Finally, there is a need for appropriate use of translators. There is a telling example of this in an account by Central Birmingham CHC (1979: 3) of a visit by their Asian representative to a local hospital. She was

> immediately asked to help [by several Asian patients] to interpret to nursing staff. In one case . . . the patient's fears were eased and she happily agreed to have an injection. In . . . another instance, a patient was anxious that she should not be discharged on that day, as intended, since she did not feel strong enough to cope with the large family and guests waiting for her at home. Thanks to the Group member's intervention, her discharge was postponed by a day or two. If three cases such as these can arise on a chance visit by a CHC member, then there must be a concern about what happens when no such person is available.

Unfortunately, there is still a widespread shortfall in the provision of adequate interpreting services, resulting not only in unmet need and inadequate or insensitive treatment as far as service users are concerned, but also in frustrating delays and other inefficiencies from the practitioners' point of view. It is vitally important to recognize that effective translation services are not an expensive luxury but, if employed appropriately, help save time and may in some cases reduce avoidable costly treatment or further unnecessary intervention.

If some form of translating service is available, practitioners are advised to check that translators actually are communicating effectively with patients or clients: whether they are fluent in the appropriate languages, for example, or whether the client or patient is comfortable with the translator (Mares *et al.* 1985: 70). Working effectively with a translator calls for the acquisition of skills and should not be seen as a simple or impromptu solution to communication problems. Above all, practitioners should try to avoid the temptation of calling upon colleagues to translate because they happen to be members of minority ethnic communities. Such colleagues have their own work to do and are not employed to be translators 'on the cheap'.

Personal care
Personal care and helping older people maintain control over their care is a key aspect of developing a good relationship. This is especially so where special culturally related care needs are concerned. The practitioner's credibility depends on his/her ability to respond to individuals' concerns about care, and if necessary to push other practitioners or carers into an awareness of these personal needs.

Personal care raises a great many practical concerns and we can do no more here than identify what seem to be leading issues, remembering – as with communication skills – that the guidelines and publications which advise on practice, discussed above, are available. Many problems can be averted by the employment and appropriate training of care staff who are members of the various minority ethnic groups, though an unthinking policy of 'ethnic matching' of staff with minority patients or clients – and no other support – can lead to yet other difficulties: the fact that an older Asian speaks the same language as home care staff, for example, does not mean that the recipient of care is automatically pleased to see someone from her own community tidy her home, or help her dress, or give her food.

Sensitivities surrounding intimate physical and personal contact are an important consideration for all practitioners, whether from a minority community or not. Managing personal hygiene or cleanliness, for example, is a concern for anyone experiencing a serious illness or a disabling condition. But there may be additional worries among older people in minority ethnic groups, for instance if there are customary procedures for cleaning and oiling hair, or if it is not customary to use the right hand to clean oneself, or if baths are considered to be polluting whereas showers are not. Tasks such as lifting involve intimate physical contact and, if non-family members do this, the feelings of the older person need every consideration; this is even more the case if help is needed with toileting – especially as attitudes to and uses of the Western WC vary, as do methods of cleaning oneself. For some older people, being clean is more than a physical state – it is a ritual necessity for prayer among Muslims, for example, and a devout person will be greatly worried if he/she is incontinent, or has been cleaned or attended to the 'wrong' way.

Being frail or dependent on others for care not only poses threats to one's dignity or status in the home, or to modesty and perceptions of cleanliness, but also to one's control over personal possessions. Older people in minority ethnic groups may badly need an ally to explain their concerns about jewellery or other treasured heirlooms (especially if these have to be removed in hospital or in a nursing home), or their wishes as far as clothing is concerned, or – for women – makeup. As far as is possible, the sensitive practitioner should find out about such concerns before an older person becomes an in-patient or a 'resident', but they may also need to be addressed even if the client or patient is receiving domiciliary care.

No mention of personal care would be complete without a reminder about food and minority needs. Again, there are clear guides to the main differences among the various communities as far as dietary habits, favoured and 'taboo' foods are concerned (Henley 1979; Shukla 1991). But in terms of developing a personal relationship, the provision of food in an acceptable way can play a leading role in establishing trust. It is very important to move beyond the question of whether the ingredients are right, or whether the food has an acceptable taste. These things are crucial, but of even greater significance are two further questions: *who* prepared the food, and *how* it was prepared (in relation to religious stipulations). Unless the practitioner can provide convincing and reassuring answers to these questions, some older people will not be able to accept the food. And as with the points relating to personal care, preparatory work by the practitioner is extremely valuable: for example, if an older person is going into hospital, the benefit of relatives bringing food to the ward can be emphasized in discussions with hospital staff, or the patient can be helped in advance to put on a list the foods he/she may not eat.

Evaluating the relationship

As part of their professional training, health and social service workers are taught how to draw a line between effective intervention at the personal level and becoming 'over-involved'. Friendliness and concern are considered appropriate, but a certain detachment is seen as necessary. Perhaps this reflects the value Western cultures attach to specialized roles and functional relationships: even though practitioners involve themselves in the most personal and intimate details of clients'/patients' lives, it is assumed that such relationships can be 'bracketed off' from the other world of reciprocal and emotional ties – the world of kinship and friendship.

Though no one would argue that practitioners should jettison the idea of retaining some detachment and impartiality – after all, these are essential for an honest and objective appraisal of one's work – we would suggest that such notions of Western professionalism are examined from the point of view of older Asian and Afro-Caribbean people. What are the implications, for example, when a personal relationship comes to an end, or a 'case' is closed? Perhaps major obstacles were encountered when the social worker or district nurse began to seek involvement with the family. If these were successfully overcome, and if consequently a bond has formed between the older person and the practitioner, it may be hard for that person – particularly if he/she is from a traditional Asian family – to learn that the relationship can simply be terminated at that point. Moreover, the family may have trusted the practitioner with important decisions and 'family affairs': the practitioner has entered into a relationship with a family, not just one individual. As Henley (1979) points out, effective work with Asian patients often involves discussion with family members, or allowing time for relatives to consult with one another. What are the feelings of relatives when a practitioner simply vanishes from the scene?

Several practical lessons might be drawn from examining these questions. First, in evaluating the impact of practitioners' personal relationships with Asian and Afro-Caribbean older people, it would seem to be important to try to keep in touch with at least a proportion of the individuals and families on one's caseload – and especially those for whom a sudden departure by the practitioner will be problematic. This point is made with the realization that there are often enormous pressures on the time available to practitioners. However, without some efforts to keep in touch, or to reinvolve older people's families in evaluating the services being provided, some practitioners will continue with a rather narrow vision of what they have achieved or what their impact has been at the personal level. The brisk cheerfulness of the professional practitioner on whirlwind visits must be challenged.

Secondly, there would seem to be benefits in trying to evaluate face-to-face relationships by involving representatives of minority communities, local voluntary organizations and other groups in discussions about general problems or questions concerning personal contacts. Rather than seeing personal encounters with older black and Asian people as a disjointed series of experiences, practitioners might then be able to learn from such community representatives what the common concerns are (for example, translation services, or access to a day centre). This does not mean that practitioners would have to take every comment at face value, but in opening up a dialogue at the community level they would be better able to find out why some of their individual relationships appear to 'work', while others do not.

Finally, evaluation of work at the face-to-face level in minority ethnic communities could be a matter of group collaboration among colleagues. As we pointed out at the beginning of this section, practical advice can be misleading if it is based on overgeneralized 'cultural tips' on how to behave with members of minority ethnic groups: the most important lesson is to build up one's own 'local knowledge' of each community and its needs. But this might be done at a department, team or group level as well as by individuals: groups of practitioners could develop their own 'home-grown' practice guides, compiling a record of which kinds of intervention appear to work best, how mistakes over uses of Asian languages, names, and so on, can be avoided. A folder containing such material and a record of personal experiences would be invaluable to newcomers to a team, as long as the contents have been discussed with advisers on race/ethnic relations or checked for accuracy by community representatives (for example, has the team understood the Muslim naming system properly, are the dates of the main religious festivals correct for this year?).

Conclusion – care by the community?

How will policy changes in 'community' care affect the outlook for older black and Asian people? Though implementation of the National Health Services and Community Care Act of 1990 was postponed and it will take some years to assess its full impact, some observers (NISW 1990; Patel 1990) are sceptical of the British government's approach, mainly because neither the legislation nor the preceding discussions (Griffiths 1988) paid any significant attention to questions of multicultural provision or racial disadvantage.

These are serious flaws in the government's approach, showing strong adherence to traditional 'colour-blind' or integrationist thinking: 'the community' in all official discussions is an almost unbelievably characterless creature. However, it is also possible to see another side to the new policy. First, it is perhaps the most fundamental attempt since the welfare state was introduced to define responsibilities in community care clearly – in terms of funding, care arrangements and assessment of needs and standards. And despite earlier equivocation, it is the local authorities which have been put in the driving seat. 'Care managers' will co-ordinate the efforts of staff from both health and social services, additionally drawing on services from the private and voluntary sectors, or upon help from relatives and neighbours (the 'informal' sector).

In principle, older black and Asian people could stand to gain, rather than lose, under the new arrangements. They were often ignored under the old-style organization of social services, which either provided inappropriate services in a 'colour-blind' way or refused to enter into partnerships with voluntary and private sector agencies. To take the example of meals provision, one cannot help thinking that the principle of contracting out the supply of a wide variety of meals for older Asians with differing religious/dietary needs will be easier to accept under the new arrangements (though in practice, probably still difficult to organize).

In future, multicultural residential care or ethnically specialized homes are almost all likely to be in the voluntary sector, managed by independent trusts, or in the private sector. As the community care reforms give incentives, through funding arrangements, for local authorities to offer places in private and voluntary homes rather than in the authorities' own accommodation, the chances of obtaining appropriate or 'ethnically sensitive' residential accommodation in these sectors could grow. The example of sheltered accommodation points the way: here, voluntary bodies – housing associations and organizations such as Asian Sheltered and Residential Accommodation – have been much more responsive than statutory housing or social services departments.

To sum up, it could be suggested that the social needs of minority ethnic groups were always expected to be solved by self-reliance rather than government action. Financial constraints on social services have been tightening since the 1970s, so that the costs of developing a complex, ethnically diverse range of *statutory* services were always unlikely to have been met.

However, there are still strong doubts about whether, or how far, the community care reforms will benefit the minorities. To begin with, it is likely that implementation will be at a gradual pace rather than overnight. Local authorities simply do not have the resources to achieve their objectives quickly. In addition, the new roles and tasks of the various players in the community care drama will have to be worked out gradually; far from eliminating confusion, new ambiguities and uncertainties about 'who does what?' will arise.

There are more fundamental questions to be asked in relation to the position of older black and Asian people themselves. First, is there a community 'out there'? In the Griffiths (1988) Report, one finds a discussion much influenced by ideas of untapped reserves of care, as if carers have been waiting for years to be given the right signal to come forward. But as Rowland (1991) points out in relation to Australia's population of ethnic minority older people, these are often the people less likely to have developed supportive relationships outside their own family or locality. As we have seen, some – for example, Asian women who cannot speak English – become dependent on a very narrow family group. Others, such as Afro-Caribbeans living alone, live in a loose-knit network rather than a closely bonded community. So, while community *is* a strong support as far as some older black and Asian people are concerned, we are nowhere near a position of 'cohort self-sufficiency' (Rowland 1991: 56) in any community. For this to occur, years of preparatory and preventive work will be required: for example, wider English learning opportunities for Asians now in middle age; better information for the pre-retirement cohort on social security and other ways of raising income in old age, such as private pension schemes; and greater involvement of 'community leaders' (in the business world as well as in politics or social life) in helping to fund and organize day centres and sheltered housing, etc.

Second, is the voluntary sector sufficiently well developed? Our review of the achievement of Caribbean and Asian voluntary groups showed that many are doing valuable work. But they are underdeveloped as a result of lack of funds, other facilities and resources, and of staff training. Their services are patchy and cannot help but perpetuate certain forms of inequality. There are emergent differences between ethnic communities, some of which are beginning to follow a 'Jewish' model of care for older people (for example, the East African Asians), while others, such as the Bangladeshi community, which are poorer, have almost no voluntary sector services for older people.

Local authority purchasing arrangements could well stimulate a flow of extra funds into services for older black and Asian people. However, there is a danger that the relatively small minority organizations will lose out to the larger national charities in the way contracts are issued or obtained (Patel 1990). Much will depend on the degree to which black representatives are involved in the initial discussions and partnerships forged between local authorities and major care providers. But even if minority voluntary organizations do obtain a fair share of the cake, it is likely that not much will change because they will still have to limp into an uncertain future on temporary contracts and limited budgets.

In view of this, the future welfare of older black and Asian people will have to rest increasingly on group strategies within the ethnic communities themselves. Community activism and mobilization, hitherto much concerned with such questions as citizenship, immigration, relations with the police, jobs, or schooling, will need to incorporate new and rather unfamiliar concerns such as preparing for retirement, lobbying for social facilities for older people and building new support networks for those who, up to now, have been constrained by housebound or home-centred ways of life.

9

Conclusion

We have sought, in this book, to highlight the growing importance of ethnic and racial dimensions in ageing. As Rowland (1991: 59) concludes: 'Such attention is warranted, not because the ethnic aged are problem groups, but because they are groups with problems which are not adequately addressed through research on the aged population as a whole'.

Rather than seeing research and practical intervention as rival or mutually exclusive activities, we have tried to stress their interdependence. Research can sometimes be a substitute for action, but in the field of minority ageing there is not much evidence of this. Comparative study (cross-racial and cross-ethnic) and the development of theory are still at a very early stage and, being small-scale, research to date has hardly drained resources from service provision. Quite the opposite: there is evidence that unless public attention is drawn to minority ageing, neither academic gerontology nor those who control resources and services will pay much heed to racial and ethnic diversity.

The road ahead, we suggest, should therefore be more of a two-lane highway than a fork, or choice, between research and intervention. In the research lane and as far as social gerontology is concerned, ethnic diversity poses a number of challenges and controversial questions.

The dominant theories on ageing – for example, disengagement theory (Cumming and Henry 1961), activity theory (Lemmon *et al.* 1976), biographical and life-history perspectives (Johnson 1976; Coleman 1986) and the political economy approach (Phillipson 1982) – need to be reconsidered with ethnic and racial diversity in mind. This would have consequences not only for our understanding of ageing in minority ethnic groups (for example, in what circumstances does retirement lead to restriction of roles and structural dependency among older people in various Asian and black communities?), but also for our views on the value of the theories themselves.

Disengagement theory, for example, has already been questioned because its claims to be universal appear to be based on fieldwork among a group which was rather narrow in cultural terms: a sample of middle-income, golf-playing, white older people living in the US Mid-West (Hochschild 1975). Disengagement may have value as a concept, as a way of understanding stages of development and of 'withdrawal from the world' in a number of cultures, but only if it is applied in a testable way with ethnic differences in mind.

The political economy perspective on the construction of old age in 'capitalist society' has had greater impact in gerontology in recent years and continues to provide insights into the nature of problems such as poverty, dependency and marginalization (see, for example, Townsend 1986). But just as the political economy perspective is challenged, if not invalidated, by striking *national* differences between capitalist societies (for example, in policies on retirement age, value of pensions and provision of services), so we must also take into account the 'internal' differentiation of capitalist society: ethnic differences and persistent racial inequalities are a key aspect of this. As the debate about double jeopardy shows, some aspects of ethnic identity have a protective influence, possibly reducing the dependency-inducing effects of institutionalized retirement; but in other respects ethnic traditions impose constraints and, notably in health and in access to social services, racial divisions seem to compound inequalities of social class.

We have shown that ethnicity and race do make a difference to the experience of ageing, whether this is in connection with preferred lifestyles and expectations of old age, roles in the family and residence patterns, gender and independence, culture-specific needs for care by voluntary and statutory services, or problems of racism and stereotyping.

And though the 'migrant generation' of older Asians and Afro-Caribbeans form unique cohorts, ethnicity and race will not necessarily dwindle in importance as they pass on. The meanings attached to being third-generation 'black', or 'Asian', or of Jamaican or Gujarati descent, will change in future years. But the experiences of older people in other ethnic communities suggest that even after a lifetime of adjustment, significant needs for 'roots', for ethnic-specific social activities, company and use of language can re-emerge or become 'resurgent' (Kastenbaum 1979). Some suggest that the significance of ethnicity to self-identity varies, waxing and waning at different points in the life course (Rowland 1991: 9).

Despite the continuing significance of race and ethnicity and the growing official acceptance of them as legitimate expressions of identity, we conclude that it will be vitally important to stimulate an open traffic of ideas between 'ethnic' or minority studies and other branches of gerontology, as well as between practitioners who deal mainly with older people in minority groups and those who do not.

It is understandable that, in societies where 'ethnic politics' matters, or where there are much larger minority communities than those in Britain, commentators have sought to define a separate field of 'ethnogerontology' (Markides 1983). But though this may help focus attention on such questions as double jeopardy and the social problems faced by particular minorities, the long-term effect is likely to be one of cutting off minority studies in a 'research ghetto', while making it more difficult to incorporate ethnic and racial comparisons in 'mainstream' gerontological research (Rowland 1991: 59).

It is possible to see the effects of this mental apartheid in relation to social class and the political economy perspective, as mentioned above, and especially if ethnicity is thought of as 'essentially cultural and existing separately from, even if closely intertwined with, social class' (Gelfand and Kutzik 1979: 357). As these authors add:

> not only is the priority of class or ethnicity a false issue, but questions can be raised as to the soundness of dealing with ethnicity in isolation from class and vice versa. Such a position led Milton Gordon (1964) to invent the term *ethclass*.
>
> (1979: 357)

If these points are true for research, they are also applicable in practice. As we noted in the chapter on welfare, there is a danger of the marginalization of minority voluntary group providers. But 'mainstream' providers have much to learn from innovative work done by black and Asian self-help groups. Equally, there are training needs among black and minority organizations, which could benefit from practice developments in the mainstream: for example, strategies to empower older people and avoid over-protectiveness, to introduce methods of countering discrimination against women, or using reminiscence work to relieve depression.

Black and Asian older people therefore face a future which is uncertain but which has the potential for a rewarding old age as well as for continuing racial inequality and other problems. Can the image of the 'passive victim' now be cast aside like temporary scaffolding, along with that of the 'self-reliant pioneer' and the 'gradually adjusting migrant'?

It may be wrong to remove the scaffolding until we learn more about minority ageing in Britain. For instance, though the word 'passive' should be rejected – there are plenty of examples of older Asian and Afro-Caribbean people who have demonstrated both self-reliance and gradual adjustment – it is worth pausing over the 'victim' image: does it perhaps have some value in depicting the outcome of ageing – not only among minority ethnic groups, but often among older people in the majority, too?

But 'victim' is a term that carries associations of helplessness and weakness. Its 'pathological overtones and emphasis on needs' (Fennell *et al.* 1988: 8) reinforce a particular stereotype of older people. We conclude, however, that older black people can appropriately be seen as victims of circumstances if such an image is coupled with a concept of *vulnerability*.

The trees of the world's rain forests are strong, mature, and diverse – but, growing on thin soils, they are extremely vulnerable to exploitation and destruction. We feel that this image illustrates the vulnerable or precarious position of many older black and Asian people quite well. Many are resourceful, well-adjusted to their position and in relatively good health. But changing circumstances can precipitate them into sudden losses of self-determination, identity or health – perhaps even more quickly than would occur among the majority. This is because, as Rowland (1991: 43) points out, 'Some of the problems of the ethnic aged are not age-specific problems at all'.

An old ex-serviceman, 2nd Battalion Sikh Pioneers, holds a portrait photograph of himself at a younger age
Photograph: John Reardon

Those in minorities face the additional problems we have discussed in this book: problems arising from racial, cultural and economic differences and disadvantages.

We should end, however, on a note that takes diversity seriously. Just as it will be necessary to jettison such general images of older black people as 'the gradually adjusting migrant' or the 'self-reliant pioneer', so it will be important to go beyond the umbrella terms of 'Asian' or 'South Asian', and 'Afro-Caribbean'. While we must never lose sight of across-the-board influences, such as race or age discrimination, upon the experience of everyone in the minority communities, it is increasingly likely that social divergence will occur between the various Asian, Afro-Caribbean and other minority communities.

At the same time, social divisions among older people as a whole are widening. These will cut across and complicate the racial and ethnic differences we have highlighted. Though there never was a common status in old age in industrial society, the uneven spread of occupational pension schemes and other changes are leading to increasing fragmentation and inequality. The frontiers of old age faced by black and Asian people involve possibilities of widening gaps between winners and losers, between affluent and not so well-off communities, and between older people who are sustained by ethnic identity and their communities and those who are not.

Bibliography

Abrams, M. (1978) *Beyond Three Score and Ten – A First Report on a Survey of the Elderly*. Mitcham, Surrey, Age Concern.

AFFOR (All Faiths for One Race) (1981) Unpublished data from survey of elders of minority ethnic groups. Handsworth, Birmingham.

Allen, S. (1982) Perhaps a seventh person? In Husband, C. (ed.), *Race in Britain: Continuity and Change*. London, Hutchinson.

Angelou, M. (1986) *And Still I Rise*. London, Virago Press.

Antonovsky, A. and Bernstein, J. (1977) Social class and infant mortality, *Social Science and Medicine*, 11, 453–70.

Anwar, M. (1979) *The Myth of Return: Pakistanis in Britain*. London, Heinemann.

Balarajan, R. and Yuen, P. (1984) Patterns of mortality among immigrants in England and Wales, *British Medical Journal*, 289, 237–9.

Barker, J. (1984) *Black and Asian Old People in Britain*. Mitcham, Surrey, Age Concern.

Baxter, C., Larbie, J. and Mares, P. (1986) *A Training Handbook for Multiracial Health Care*. Cambridge, National Extension College.

Beevers, D. G. (1981) Ethnic differences in common diseases, *Postgraduate Medical Journal*, 57(674), 744.

Bengston, V. L. (1979) Ethnicity and aging: problems and issues in current social science enquiry. In Gelfand, D. E. and Kutzik, A. J. (eds), *Ethnicity and Aging*. New York, Springer.

Berry, S., Lee, M. and Griffiths, S. (1981) *Report on a Survey of West Indian Pensioners in Nottingham*. Social Services Research Section, Nottingham City Council.

Bhachu, P. (1985) *Twice Migrants: East African Settlers in Britain*. London, Tavistock.

Bhalla, A. and Blakemore, K. (1981) *Elders of the Minority Ethnic Groups*. AFFOR, Birmingham.

Blakemore, K. (1982) Health and illness among the elderly of minority ethnic groups, *Health Trends*, 14(3), 68–72.

Blakemore, K. (1983a) Their needs are different, *Community Care*, 10 February, 12–13.

Blakemore, K. (1983b) Ethnicity, self-reported illness and use of medical services by the elderly, *Postgraduate Medical Journal*, 59, 45–7.

Blakemore, K. (1983c) Ageing in the inner city – a comparison of old blacks and whites. In Jerrome, D. (ed.), *Ageing in Modern Society*. London, Croom Helm.

Blakemore, K. (1984) Unpublished interviews, follow-up survey of respondents in the AFFOR (1981) sample, Birmingham.

Blakemore, K. (1985a) Ethnic inequalities in old age: some comparisons between Britain and the United States, *Journal of Applied Gerontology*, 4(1), 86–101.

Blakemore, K. (1985b) The state, the voluntary sector and new developments in provision for the old of minority racial groups, *Ageing and Society*, 5(2), 175–90.

Boneham, M. (1987) Ethnicity and ageing in Britain: a study of elderly Sikh women in a Midlands town. PhD thesis, Centre for Urban and Regional Studies, University of Birmingham.

Boneham, M. (1989) Ageing and ethnicity in Britain: the case of elderly Sikh women in a Midlands town, *New Community*, 15(3), 447–59.

Bradshaw, J. (1972) The concept of social need, *New Society*, 30, 640–3.

Braham, P., Rhodes, E. and Pearn, M. (eds) (1981) *Discrimination and Disadvantage in Employment*. London, Harper & Row.

Brenton, M. (1985) *The Voluntary Sector in British Social Services*. London, Longman.

Brown, C. (1984) *Black and White Britain: the Third PSI Survey*. London, Heinemann.

Bulmer, M. (ed.) (1986) *Social Science and Social Policy*. London, Allen & Unwin.

Burton, L. and Bengston, V. L. (1982) Research in elderly minority communities. In Manuel, R. C. (ed.), *Minority Aging*. Westport, Connecticut, Greenwood Press.

Cameron, E., Badger, F. and Evers, H. (1989) District nursing, the disabled and the elderly: who are the black patients?, *Journal of Advanced Nursing*, 14, 376–82.

Cantor, M. H. (1976) The effect of ethnicity on life-styles of the inner-city elderly. In Lawton, M. P., Newcomer, R. J. and Byerts, T. O. (eds), *Community Planning for an Aging Society*. New York, Dowden, Hutchinson and Ross.

Cashmore, E. E. and Troyna, B. (1989) *Introduction to Race Relations*. London, Falmer Press.

Castles, S. and Kosack, G. (1985) *Immigrant Workers and the Class Structure in Western Europe*, 2nd edn. London, Oxford University Press.

Central Birmingham CHC (1979) Client group review 4: Asian patients. Unpublished Paper, Central Birmingham Community Health Council.

Central Statistical Office (1980) *Social Trends, No. 10*. London, HMSO.

Chiu, S. (1989) Chinese elderly people: no longer a treasure at home, *Social Work Today*, 10 August, 15–17.

Cochrane, R. and Rowe, M. (1980) The mental health of immigrants, *New Community*, 8, 123–9.

Coleman, P. (1986) *The Ageing Process and the Role of Reminiscence*. London, John Wiley.

Commission for Racial Equality (1978) *Multi-Racial Britain: the Social Services Response*. Working Party Report, London, CRE.

Connelly, N. (1989) *Race and Change in Social Service Departments*. London, Policy Studies Institute.

Cool, L. E. (1980) Ethnic identity: a source of community esteem for the elderly, *Anthropological Quarterly*, 54, 179–81.

Cool, L. E. (1981) Ethnicity and aging – continuity through change in elderly Corsicans. In Fry, C. (ed.), *Community Planning for an Aging Society*. New York, Dowden, Hutchinson and Ross.

Copeland, J. R. M. (1988) Quantifying clinical observation – Geriatric Mental State (AGECAT package). In Wattis, J. P. and Hindmarch, I. (eds), *Psychological Assessments of the Elderly*. Edinburgh, Churchill Livingstone.

Coventry City Council (1986) Unpublished data, Ethnic Minorities Elders' Survey, Coventry Social Services Department.

Cowgill, D. O. (1974) Aging and modernization: A revision of the theory. In Gubrium,

J. (ed.), *Later Life: Communities and Environmental Policy*. Springfield, Ill., Charles Thomas.

Cowgill, D. O. (1986) *Aging Around the World*. Belmont, California, Wadsworth.

Cowgill, D. O. and Holmes, D. (eds) (1972) *Aging and Modernization*. New York, Appleton-Century-Crofts.

Cross, M. (1987) The black economy, *New Society*, 81, 24 July, 16–19.

Cross, M. and Entzinger, H. (eds) (1988) *Lost Illusions: Caribbean Minorities in Britain and the Netherlands*. London, Routledge.

Cruickshank, J. K., Beevers, D. G., Osbourne, V. L., Haynes, R. A., Corlett, J. C. R. and Selby, S. (1980) Heart attack, stroke, diabetes and hypertension in West Indians, Asians and whites in Birmingham, England, *British Medical Journal*, 281, 25 October, 1108.

Cumming, E. and Henry, W. E. (1961) *Growing Old: The Process of Disengagement*. New York, Basic Books.

Daniel, S. (1988) A code to care for elders, *Social Work Today*, 19(50), 9.

Darby, S. J. (1989) Health needs of ethnic elderly people, *Health Visitor*, 62(10), 304–5.

Delaney, S. (1959) *A Taste of Honey*. London, Methuen.

Department of Health and Social Security (1978) *A Happier Old Age*. London, HMSO.

Dhanjal, B. (1976) Sikh women in Southall, *New Community*, 5(1–2), 109–17.

Donaldson, L. J. (1986) Health and social status of elderly Asians: a community survey, *British Medical Journal*, 293, 1079–84.

Donovan, J. (1984) Ethnicity and health: a research review, *Social Science and Medicine*, 19(7), 663–670.

Donovan, J. (1986) *We Don't Buy Sickness, it Just Comes*. Aldershot, Gower.

Dowd, J. (1980) *Stratification among the Aged*. Monterey, California, Brooks-Cole.

Dowd, J. J. and Bengston, V. L. (1978) Aging in minority populations – an examination of the double jeopardy hypothesis, *Journal of Gerontology*, 33, 427–36.

Driedger, L. and Chappell, N. (1987) *Aging and Ethnicity: Towards an Interface*. Toronto, Butterworths.

Ebrahim, S., Smith, C. and Giggs, J. (1987) Elderly immigrants – a disadvantaged group?, *Age and Ageing*, 16(4), 249–55.

Ebrahim, S., Patel, N., Coats, M., Greig, C., Gilley, J., Bangham, C. and Stacey, S. (1991) Prevalence and severity of morbidity among Gujarati Asian elders: a controlled comparison, *Family Practice*, 8(1), 57–62.

Edwards, J. (1987) *Positive Discrimination, Social Justice and Social Policy*. London, Tavistock.

Eribo, L. (1991) *The Support You Need – Information for Carers of Afro-Caribbean People*. London, King's Fund Centre.

EURAG (1987) *The Older Migrant*. The Hague, European Association for the Welfare of the Elderly.

Eyer, J. (1980) Hypertension as a disease of modern society. In Mechanic, D. (ed.), *Readings in Medical Sociology*. New York, Free Press.

Fennell, G., Phillipson, C. and Evers, H. (1988) *The Sociology of Old Age*. Milton Keynes, Open University Press.

Fenton, S. (1986) *Race, Health and Welfare: Afro-Caribbean and South Asian People in Central Bristol*. Department of Sociology, University of Bristol.

Fenton, S. (1987) *Ageing Minorities: Black People as they Grow Old in Britain*. London, Commission for Racial Equality.

Flannery, E. (1981) Ethnicity as a factor in the expression of pain, *Psychosomatics*, 22 January, 39–50.

Foner, N. (1973) *Status and Power in Rural Jamaica*. New York, Teachers College Press.

Foner, N. (1979) *Jamaica Farewell*. London, Routledge.

Fryer, P. (1984) *Staying Power: The History of Black People in Britain*. London, Pluto Press.

Gelfand, D. E. and Kutzik, A. J. (eds) (1979) *Ethnicity and Aging*. New York, Springer.

Gilbert, J. (1988) Excellence in ethnic elder care, *Social Work Today*, 19(23), 18–19.

Glazer, N. and Moynihan, D. (1975) *Ethnicity: Theory and Experience*. London, Harvard University Press.

Glendenning, F. (ed.) (1979) *The Elders in Ethnic Minority Groups*. Keele, Beth Johnson Foundation and Department of Adult Education, University of Keele.

Glendenning, F. and Pearson, M. (1988) *The Black and Ethnic Minority Elders in Britain: Health Needs and Access to Services*. Health Education Authority/Centre for Social Gerontology, University of Keele.

Gordon, M. (1964) *Assimilation in American Life*. New York, Oxford University Press.

Griffiths, R. (1988) *Community Care: Agenda for Action*. London, HMSO.

Harlan, W. H. (1964) Social status of the aged in three Indian villages, *Vita Humana*, 7, 239–52.

Haskey, J. (1991) The ethnic minority populations resident in private households, *Population Trends*, Spring, 22–35.

Hazan, H. (1980) *The Limbo People: a Study of the Constitution of the Time Universe among the Aged*. London, Routledge & Kegan Paul.

Henley, A. (1979) *Asian Patients in Hospital and at Home*. London, King Edward's Hospital Fund.

Henley, A. and Taylor, C. (1986) *Asians in Britain Series*. Cambridge, National Extension College.

Hochschild, A. R. (1975) Disengagement theory: a critique and proposal, *American Sociological Review*, 40, 553–69.

Holmes, L. D. (1987) Cultural values and cultural change: a cross-cultural analysis of aging and age status, *Journal of Cross-Cultural Gerontology*, 2, 195–200.

Holzberg, C. (1982) Ethnicity and aging: anthropological perspectives on more than just the minority elderly, *The Gerontologist*, 33, 249–57.

Jackson, J. A. (1963) *The Irish in Britain*. Routledge, London.

Jackson, J. J. (1980) *Minorities and Aging*. Belmont, Wadsworth.

Jackson, M., Kolody, B. and Wood, J. L. (1982) To be old and black: the case for double jeopardy on income and health. In Manuel, R. C. (ed.), *Minority Aging*. Westport, Connecticut, Greenwood Press.

Jeffery, P. (1976) *Migrants and Refugees – Muslim and Christian Pakistani Families in Bristol*. Cambridge, Cambridge University Press.

Johnson, C. L. (1986) *Growing Up and Growing old in Italian-American Families*. New Brunswick, New Jersey, Rutgers University Press.

Johnson, Malcolm L. (1976) That was your life: a biographical approach to later life. In Munnichs, J. M. and Van Den Heuval, W. J. (eds), *Dependency and Interdependency in Old Age*. The Hague, Martinus Nijhoff.

Johnson, Mark (1984) Ethnic minorities and health, *Journal of the Royal College of Physicians*, 18(4), 228–30.

Johnson, Mark (1986) Inner city residents, ethnic minorities and primary health care in the West Midlands. In Rathwell, T. and Phillips, D. (eds), *Health, Race and Ethnicity*. London, Croom Helm.

Jones, S. (1986) The elders: a new generation, *Ageing and Society*, 6(3), 313–31.

Karseras, P. and Hopkins, E. (1987) *British Asians – Health in the Community*. London, Wiley.

Kastenbaum, R. (1979) Reflections on old age, ethnicity, and death. In Gelfand, D. E. and Kutzik, A. J. (eds), *Ethnicity and Aging*. New York, Springer.

Kent, D. (1971) The elderly in minority groups, *The Gerontologist*, 11, 26–9.

Kippax, C. (1978) *A Step into the Unknown*. Lewisham, Age Concern.

Kuper, A. (1976) *Changing Jamaica*. London, Routledge & Kegan Paul.

Larson, R. (1978) Thirty years of research on the subjective wellbeing of the older American, *Journal of Gerontology*, 33, 109–29.

Laslett, P. (1976) Societal development and aging. In Binstock, R. H. and Shanas, E. (eds), *Handbook of Aging and the Social Sciences*. New York, Van Nostrand Reinhold.

Lemmon, B., Bengston, V. and Peterson, J. (1976) An explanation of the activity theory of aging. In Bell, B. (ed.), *Contemporary Social Gerontology*, Springfield, Illinois, Charles Thomas.

Lieberman, S. and Au, S. (1988) Catering for a minority, *Community Care*, 10 November, 737, 20–22.

Little, K. (1947) *Negroes in Britain*. London, Kegan Paul, Trench, Trubner & Co.

Littlewood, R. and Cross, S. (1980) Ethnic minorities and psychiatric services, *Sociology of Health and Illness*, 2(2), 194–201.

Littlewood, R. and Lipsedge, M. (1982) *Aliens and Alienists*. Harmondsworth, Penguin.

Liu, W. T. (1986) Health services for Asian elderly, *Research on Aging*, 8(1), 156–75.

Liverpool Personal Service Society (1988) *Supported Group Living for Ethnic Elders*. 34 Stanley Street, Liverpool.

Lowenthal, D. (1972) *West Indian Societies*. London, Oxford University Press.

Lowenthal, D. and Comitas, L. (1973) *Consequences of Class and Color – West Indian Perspectives*. New York, Anchor Press/Doubleday.

McCalman, J. A. (1990) *The Forgotten People – Carers in Three Minority Ethnic Communities in Southwark*. London, King's Fund Centre/Help the Aged.

McFarland, E., Dalton, M. and Walsh, D. (1989) Ethnic minority needs and service delivery: the barriers to access in a Glasgow inner-city area, *New Community*, 15(3), 405–15.

McKeown, T. (1979) *The Role of Medicine*, 2nd edn. Oxford, Blackwell.

McNaught, A. (1984) *Race and Health Care in the U.K.* Centre for Health Service Management Studies, Polytechnic of the South Bank, London.

McNaught, A. (1988) *Race and Health Policy*. London, Croom Helm.

Manton, K. G. (1982) Differential life expectancy: possible explanations during the later ages. In Manuel, R. C. (ed.), *Minority Aging*, Westport, Connecticut, Greenwood Press.

Manuel, R. C. (1982) The dimensions of ethnic minority identification. In Manuel, R. C. (ed.), *Minority Aging*. Westport, Connecticut, Greenwood Press.

Mares, P., Henley, A. and Baxter, C. (1985) *Health Care in Multiracial Britain*. Cambridge, Health Education Council and National Extension College.

Markides, K. (1982) Ethnicity and aging – a comment, *The Gerontologist*, 22, 467–72.

Markides, K. (1983) Minority aging. In Riley, M., Hess, B. B. and Bond, K. (eds), *Aging in Society: Selected Reviews of Recent Research*. Hillsdale, New Jersey, Erlbaum Inc.

Markides, K. and Mindel, C. H. (1987) *Aging and Ethnicity*. Newbury Park, California, Sage.

Marmot, M. G., Adelstein, A. and Bulusu, L. (1983) Immigrant mortality in England and Wales, *Population Trends*, 33, 14–17.

Marmot, M. G., Adelstein, A. and Bulusu, L. (1984) Immigrant mortality in England and Wales, 1970–78: causes of death by country of birth. In *Studies on Medical and Population Subjects, No. 47*. HMSO, London.

May, R. and Cohen, R. (1974) The interaction between race and colonialism: a case study of the Liverpool race riots of 1919, *Race and Class*, 16(2), 111–26.

Mays, N. (1983) Elderly south Asians in Britain: a survey of the relevant literature and themes for future research, *Ageing and Society*, 3, 71–97.

Nagi, S. and Haavio-Mannila, E. (1980) Migration, health status and utilisation of health services, *Sociology of Health and Illness*, 2(2), 174–93.

Nanton, P. (1992) Official statistics and the problem of inappropriate ethnic categorisation, *Policy and Politics*, 20(4), 277–86.

National Extension College (1986) Foods and diets in a multiracial society, *Health and Race*, July/August, issue no. 6 (*Training on Health and Race*). Leeds, NEC.

National Urban League (1964) *Double Jeopardy, the Older Negro in America Today*. New York, National Urban League.

NISW (National Institute for Social Work) (1990) *Black Community and Community Care*. London, Race Equality Unit, NISW.

Norman, A. (1985) *Triple Jeopardy: Growing Old in a Second Homeland*. London, Centre for Policy on Ageing.

Oberg, K. (1954) *Culture Shock*. Indianapolis, Bobbs-Merrill.

O'Connor, K. (1972) *The Irish in Britain*. London, Sidgwick & Jackson.

Office of Population Censuses and Surveys (1982) *International Migration*, Statistical Series MN. 9. London, HMSO.

Office of Population Censuses and Surveys (1983) *Census 1981: Country of Birth – Great Britain*. London, HMSO.

Office of Population Censuses and Surveys (1991) *Labour Force Survey 1988 and 1989*. London, HMSO.

Ogbu, J. U. (1978) *Minority Education and Caste*. New York, Academic Press.

Palmore, E. (1983) Cross-cultural research: state of the art, *Research on Aging*, 5, 45–57.

Palmore, E. and Maeda, D. (1985) *The Honorable Elders Revisited*. Durham, North Carolina, Duke University Press.

Patel, N. (1990) *A 'Race' Against Time?* London, The Runnymede Trust.

Patrick, D. L. and Scambler, G. (eds) (1986) *Sociology as Applied to Medicine*, 2nd edn. Eastbourne, Bailliere-Tindall.

Patterson, S. (1965) *Dark Strangers – a Study of West Indians in London*. Harmondsworth, Penguin.

Peach, C. (1991) *The Caribbean in Europe: Contrasting Patterns of Migration and Settlement in Britain, France and the Netherlands*, Research Paper No. 15. Centre for Research in Ethnic Relations, University of Warwick.

Pearson, M. (1986) The politics of ethnic minority health studies. In Rathwell, T. and Phillips, D. (eds), *Health, Race and Ethnicity*. London, Croom Helm.

Peil, M. (1985) Old age in West Africa: social support and quality of life. In Morgan, J. H. (ed.), *Aging in Developing Societies, Vol. 2*. Bristol, Indiana, Wyndham Hall Press.

Peil, M. (1987) Review article: studies of ageing in Africa, *Ageing and Society*, 7, 459–66.

Pharoah, C. and Redmond, E. (1991) Care for ethnic elders, *Health Service Journal*, 16 May, 101, 5252, 20–2.

Phillipson, C. (1982) *Capitalism and the Construction of Old Age*. London, Macmillan.

Pilkington, A. (1984) *Race Relations in Britain*. London, University Tutorial Press.

Powles, J. (1980) On the limitations of modern medicine. In Mechanic, D. (ed.), *Readings in Medical Sociology*. New York, Free Press.

Pryce, K. (1986) *Endless Pressure – a Study of West Indian Lifestyles in Bristol*, 2nd edn. Bristol, Bristol Classical Press.

Rack, P. (1982) *Race, Culture and Mental Disorder*. London, Tavistock.

Rampton, A. (1981) *West Indian Children in Our Schools*, Cmnd 8273. (The Rampton Report). HMSO.

Randhawa, M. (1993) Personal communication, City of Birmingham Social Services Department.

Rathwell, T. and Phillips, D. (1986) *Health, Race and Ethnicity*. London, Croom Helm.

Rees, S. (1978) *Social Work Face to Face*. London, Edward Arnold.

Refugee Action (1987) *Last Refuge: Elderly People from Vietnam in the U.K.* Derby.

Reid, J. (1985) Going up or 'going down': the status of old people in an Australian Aboriginal Society, *Ageing and Society*, 5, 69–95.

Rex, J. (1986) *Race and Ethnicity*. Milton Keynes, Open University Press.

Rex, J. and Moore, R. (1967) *Race, Community and Conflict*. London, Oxford University Press.

Roberts, E. C. (1957) Redevelopment at Butetown North, *The Municipal Journal*, 8 February, 297–8.

Rose, E. J. B., Deakin, N., Abrams, M., Jackson, V., Peston, M., Vanagi, A., Cohen, B., Gaitskell, J. and Ward, P. (1969) *Colour and Citizenship: A Report on British Race Relations*. London, Oxford University Press.

Rosenthal, C. J. (1983) Aging, ethnicity and the family: beyond the modernization thesis, *Canadian Ethnic Studies*, 15(3), 1–16.

Rowland, D. T. (1991) *Pioneers Again: Immigrants and Ageing in Australia*. Australian Government Publishing Service, Canberra.

Rowlings, C. (1981) *Social Work with Elderly People*. London, George Allen & Unwin.

Runnymede Trust and Radical Statistics Race Group (1980) *Britain's Black Population*. London, Heinemann.

Saifullah Khan, V. S. (1976) Pakistani women in Britain, *New Community*, 5(1–2), 99–117.

Saifullah Khan, V. S. (1982) The role of the culture of dominance in structuring the experience of ethnic minorities. In Husband, C. (ed.), *'Race' in Britain*. London, Hutchinson.

Schaie, K. W., Orchowsky, S. and Parham, I. A. (1982) Measuring age and sociocultural change: the case of race and life satisfaction. In Manuel, R. C. (ed.), *Minority Aging*. Westport, Connecticut, Greenwood Press.

Shaw, A. (1988) *A Pakistani Community in Britain*. Oxford, Blackwell.

Shukla, K. (1991) Nutrition and dietetics. In Squires, A. (ed.), *Multicultural Health Care and Rehabilitation of Older People*. London, Edward Arnold.

Silman, A., Evans, S. and Loysen, E. (1987) Blood pressure and migration: a study of Bengali immigrants in East London, *Journal of Epidemiology and Community Health*, 41, 152–5.

Simmons, L. (1945) *The Role of the Aged in Primitive Society*. London, Oxford University Press.

Smith, D. J. (1977) *Racial Disadvantage in Britain: the PEP Report*. Harmondsworth, Penguin.

Smith, M. G. (1973) Education and occupational choice in rural Jamaica. In Lowenthal, D. and Comitas, L. (eds), *Consequences of Class and Color – West Indian Perspectives*. New York, Anchor Press/Doubleday.

Social Work Today (1990) Dr B's recipe for minority tastes, 14 June, 28–9.

Solomos, J. (1989) *Race and Racism in Contemporary Britain*. Basingstoke, Macmillan.

Sondhi, R. (1985) Personal communication, Asian Resource Centre, Handsworth, Birmingham.

Squires, A. (ed.) (1991) *Multicultural Health Care and Rehabilitation of Older People*. London, Edward Arnold.

Srivastava, R. P. (1974) Family organization and change among the overseas Indians, with special reference to Indian immigrant families of British Columbia, Canada. In Kurian, G. (ed.), *The Family in India – a Regional View*. The Hague, Mouton.

Stewart, M. and Whitting, G. (1983) *Ethnic Minorities and the Urban Programme*. University of Bristol, School of Advanced Urban Studies.

Stone, J. (1985) *Racial Conflict in Contemporary Society*. London, Fontana/Collins.

Stopes-Roe, M. and Cochrane, R. (1990) *Citizens of this Country: the Asian-British*. Clevedon, Multilingual Matters.

Swift, C. (1989) Health care of the elderly: the concept of progress. In Warnes, A. M. (ed.), *Human Ageing and Later Life*. London, Edward Arnold.

Tout, K. (1989) *Ageing in Developing Countries*. London, Oxford University Press.

Townsend, P. (1986) Ageism and social policy. In Phillipson, C. and Walker, A. (eds), *Ageing and Social Policy*. Aldershot, Gower.

Townsend, P. and Davidson, N. (1982) *Inequalities in Health – the Black Report*. Harmondsworth, Penguin.

Townsend, P., Davidson, N. and Whitehead, M. (1988) *Inequalities in Health: the Black Report and the Health Divide*. Harmondsworth, Penguin.

Tuckett, D., Boulton, M., Olson, C. and Williams, A. (1985) *Meetings Between Experts*. London, Tavistock.

Turnbull, A. (1985) *Greenwich's Afro-Caribbean and South Asian People*. London, Borough of Greenwich Directorate of Social Services.

van Amersfoort, H. (1982) *Immigration and the Formation of Minority Groups: the Dutch Experience 1945–75*. Cambridge, Cambridge University Press.

Vatuk, S. (1980) Withdrawal and disengagement as a cultural response to aging in India. In Fry, C. (ed.), *Aging in Culture and Society*. New York, Praeger.

Victor, C. (1987) *Old Age in Modern Society*. London, Croom Helm.

Wallman, S. (ed.) (1979) *Ethnicity at Work*. London, Macmillan.

Weightman, G. (1977) Poor man's Harley Street, *New Society*, 20 October.

Werbner, P. (1989) *The Migration Process*. New York, Berg.

Westergaard, J. and Resler, H. (1977) *Class in Capitalist Society*. Harmondsworth, Penguin.

Whitehead, M., with Townsend, P. and Davidson, N. (eds) (1988) *Inequalities in Health: the Black Report and the Health Divide*. Harmondsworth, Penguin.

Williams, J. (1990) Elders from black and minority ethnic communities. In Sinclair, I., Parker, R., Leat, D. and Williams, J. *The Kaleidoscope of Care*. London, National Institute of Social Work/HMSO.

Wilson, A. (1978) *Finding a Voice: Asian Women in Britain*. London, Virago.

Zola, I. K. (1966) Culture and symptoms – an analysis of patients' presenting complaints, *American Sociological Review*, 31, 615–30.

Index